Fergus E. Buchanan

A Journey through Suffering

Alister McGrath

Hodder & Stoughton
LONDON SYDNEY AUCKLAND

Copyright © 1992 by Alister E. McGrath

First published in Great Britain 1992. Second edition 1996

The right of Alister E. McGrath to be identified as the Author of the Work has been asserted by him in accordance with the Copyright, Designs and Patents Act 1988.

10 9 8 7 6 5 4 3 2 1

British Library Cataloguing in Publication Data
A record for this book is available from the British Library

ISBN 0 340 64173 8

Printed and bound in Great Britain by
Cox and Wyman Ltd, Reading, Berks

Hodder and Stoughton
A Division of Hodder Headline PLC
338 Euston Road
London NW1 3BH

Contents

ACKNOWLEDGEMENTS

Although the issues dealt with in this book have been on my mind for many years, I finally got round to writing it during an intensive month-long period of teaching at Ridley College, University of Melbourne, Australia, during July and August 1991. I am enormously grateful to Maurice and Jacqueline Betteridge, John and Lynn Pryor, and Bryden and Cathy Black for their hospitality and many kindnesses during my time in Australia. College secretaries Beryl Barter and Shirley Tongue cheerfully lent me their typewriters and made me coffee as I worked on the typescript of the work.

INTRODUCTION TO
THE SECOND EDITION

Suffering causes bewilderment to many Christians. It is distressing in many ways, not least on account of the pain and fear which it brings. Yet it also causes anxiety at a far deeper level. Might not suffering call into question the goodness of God? Perhaps God is not as loving and caring as we might like to think. These fears and concerns are real and must be addressed, but they need not be feared. For at its heart, the Christian faith focuses on an image of pain and suffering – the cross of Christ. Christianity does not evade the pain and sorrow of suffering. It faces it head on, declaring that God himself knows what it is like to suffer and shares in our suffering. To reflect on this theme is to open up new perspectives.

Jesus Christ suffered on the cross. This remarkable statement holds the key to a Christian understanding of suffering. None other than the son of God himself underwent pain and death. To think about the death of Christ on the cross is not merely to reflect on the place of suffering in the life of faith. It is to open up a deeper appreciation of the wonderful love and compassion of God for us, and to enable us to gain a fuller understanding of the nature of the gospel of Jesus Christ. Suffering may initially call God's goodness into question. Yet as we think more deeply on this theme, we are drawn deeper and deeper into a fuller appreciation of the wonder of all that God has done for us in Christ.

Above all, it causes us to focus on the compassion of God and the nature of Christian hope. All too often, the great theme of the resurrection of Christ is left out of our thinking about suffering. Yet the hope of resurrection must dominate our thinking here. Many years before the birth of Christ, the Greek philosopher Socrates was put to death by poisoning. He died with great dignity, an enduring example of the way in which human beings can face death with dignity. Socrates may encourage us to die with dignity; Jesus Christ enables us to die with hope, in the knowledge that suffering will have no place in the New Jerusalem.

This little book is a personal reflection on suffering, not a neat set of trite answers and pat solutions to the pain and bewilderment which suffering brings. I want to make it clear that I have no moral claims to write on this theme. I have never suffered greatly myself. But I, like many other Christians, have given much thought to the question, in the belief that it is important to think about this aspect of our faith and life. What I have done is to approach my theme from a number of different angles, trying to open out its various aspects and make some kind of response to them. Nothing more. But if what is written here helps its readers in anything like the way that the thinking behind it has helped me, it will have been more than worth while.

1

THE BALCONY AND THE ROAD

There was time to kill. I was visiting Princeton, the celebrated seat of learning in New Jersey, and found that I had an hour or so to spare before I was due to give some lectures. I decided to explore the Speer Library, one of Princeton's most famous collections of books. Browsing through its shelves, I came across John Mackey's *Preface to Christian Theology*. I had heard of Mackey before. I knew that he had once been President of Princeton Theological Seminary, and hence was likely to be worth reading. Propping myself against a row of shelves, I began to devour the book. It was not long before I found myself held captive by a superb image this man used to make one of his many memorable points.

Mackey entitles the second chapter of his work 'Two Perspectives: The Balcony and the Road'. The imagery is drawn from everyday life in the Spain of the 1920s, where Mackey spent a significant period of his life studying the Spanish language. Here is how he describes these two very different ways of looking at the problems of life:

> By the Balcony ... I mean that little platform in wood or stone that protrudes from the upper window of a Spanish home. There the family may gather of an evening to gaze spectator-wise upon the street beneath, or at the sunset or the stars beyond ...

3

By the Road, I mean the place where life is tensely lived, where thought has its birth in conflict and concern, where choices are made and decisions are carried out. It is the place of action, of pilgrimage, of crusade, where concern is never absent from a wayfarer's heart. On the Road a goal is sought, dangers are faced, life is poured out.

The two different perspectives are those of the *spectator* and of the *participant*. Those sitting comfortably on the Balcony could watch those below them as they struggle in their journey, as they get lost on the road, or as they try to work out what to do next. They need not get involved with their problems, except in a vaguely theoretical way.

Which of these two perspectives – the Balcony and the Road, the attitude of the observer and the participant – is the more important? Let us hear Mackey once more: 'Truth is found upon the Road. It might even be said that only when a man descends from the Balcony to the Road, whether of his own free will, or because he has been pitched from it by providential circumstances, does he begin to know what reality is.'

The true place of the Christian faith is on the Road. Those on the Road are facing real issues, and have to make real decisions which will affect their future and their welfare. Those on the Road cannot know what lies over the brow of the next hill, or what awaits them around the next bend. They are like people walking in the dark, and on their own.

By contrast, those on the Balcony are spared the indecision and bewilderment so often experienced by those below them, who are wondering where the Road ahead of them leads, and how likely they are to get to their intended destination. This perspective can be very helpful in understanding the divide that sometimes exists between theologians and ordinary Christian believers. At its worst, the Balcony approach involves merely noticing other people suffering. It stimulates a convivial after-dinner discussion on where suffering comes from, and a myriad of related academic issues which will occupy the diners for the remainder of a thought-provoking evening.

The problem, seen from the Road, is very different. Those on the Road are suffering, and are wondering how on earth they will cope with it, and continue the life of faith as they suffer. They are participating in suffering, not observing it at a safe distance. Their difficulties are practical, not theoretical. They need something to help them keep going on that Road. The uncommitted and detached perspective of the Balcony seems to have little bearing on their position.

But it need not be like this. Those high above the Road on the Balcony could be of help to those on the Road – above all, if they were fellow travellers, engaged on the same journey. For at its best, the Balcony perspective can be profoundly helpful. Those on the Balcony can see further, on account of their elevated position. They can see the full glory of a sunset or a starlit sky and not just the potholes and puddles; where those on the Road see only to the next bend, those on the Balcony can see where the Road is going, and what it avoids. The Balcony provides a perspective to make sense of the Road.

How? Try to enter into the world of Mackey's memorable image. Allow your imagination to conjure up that Spanish Balcony, high above a road, just after sunset on a hot and dusty day. Crowds of people are milling around on the Road, and occasionally they catch snatches of the conversation from the brightly lit Balcony above them. Now imagine the questions that might be going through their minds as they prepare to travel tonight. Which of the roads before us should we take? Where do they lead? Is it safe? What lies round that corner or over the brow of that hill?

High above the Road, those on the Balcony have over-heard the questions being asked by the travellers. They could – if they wanted to – come down from the Balcony, and be of some use to those on the Road. They could tell them of what they could see beyond the brow of the hill. They could assure them that others trudging along that Road had asked more or less the same questions, and were worried about more or less the same things. They could share with them the collected wisdom of past travellers, making the discoveries of that past available to those who need them in the present. In short, they could make the lot of those travellers much easier.

Just as the Balconeers overheard conversations from below on the Road, so the theologian can explain how Christians, from the earliest of times to the present, have wrestled with the problem of suffering. John of Salisbury, a great writer of the Middle Ages, suggested that theologians were like 'dwarves sitting on the shoulders of giants'. They were able to see more, and see further, not on account of their own greatness, but because of the stature of those upon whose shoulders they sat. To stand on that Balcony is to stand on the shoulders of generation after generation of Christian thinkers who have wrestled with these problems, which are not new. There is no need to begin all over again, for we can make them our starting point.

The theologian can allow believers of today to over-hear the conversations of the past, as the great and the good developed ways of casting light on the purpose and place of suffering in the Christian life. Those conversations can help; they need to be made available. As the great Swiss theologian Karl Barth wrote,

> We cannot be in the church without taking as much responsibility for the theology of the past as for the theology of the present. Augustine,

Thomas Aquinas, Luther, Schleiermacher and
all the rest are not dead but living. They still
speak and demand a hearing as living voices,
as surely as we know that they and we be-
long together in the church.

Just as the Balconeers had a different perspective from
those on the Road, so the theologian allows suffering to
be seen from a different vantage point. He or she will
try to place it in the context of the overall purposes of
God for believers. The Balcony can so easily become an
ivory tower, a way of escaping from the world. But as
Martin Luther pointed out, it need not, and should not.
The true theologian is one who suffers with the people
of God, and who tries to make sense of this suffering
within the purposes and providence of God. Sharing
that suffering, the theologian aims to gain a true perspective upon it, asking how it might be seen in a fresh
light, or harnessed to bring about spiritual maturity.

Those who are struggling with the life of faith need to
be consoled and reassured. Yet the consolation offered
must be genuine. It must be based on the bedrock of
Christian truth, not on the white lies of well-meant
deception. Given that suffering happens, what can be
said to those passing beneath its shadow? What consolation can be offered to them?

Theology may not be able to abolish suffering – but
it can allow that suffering to be seen in a new light.
Although the way things are cannot be changed, the
way in which people view them and respond to them
can. The theologian can reassure believers concerning
the validity of their faith, and help them to apply it
to the riddles of life. For faith makes a vital difference to the way we see and experience things. Just
as the sun shines upon the righteous and the unright-
eous, so both the believer and the non-believer suffer
and die. The vital difference lies in the way in which

they experience and understand what is happening to them.

As we shall see, the gospel allows us to think positively about suffering. The theologian can explain how this works, and reassure believers that to think positively about suffering is not to take refuge in unreality. The Christian's outlook on suffering is grounded in the self-revelation of God, and is not the product of despairing human imagination.

And finally, the theologian can reassure us that the Christian approach to suffering is *true*. How can we know that it is not just some consoling philosophy dreamed up by some idealists, who live in a pretend and make-believe world? There seems to be something within human nature which makes us trust things in inverse proportion to their value. The more momentous a promise is, the less we are likely to trust it. The more someone offers to give us, the less likely we are to believe him or her. 'There must be a catch somewhere!' The theologian can help, by reassuring those on the Road that their hope in the face of suffering and pain is for real. They show how it is grounded in the real life, death and resurrection of Jesus Christ.

Many of the theological and philosophical texts I have wrestled with seem to be much more concerned with upholding the integrity of a God who seems to allow suffering, than with saying anything helpful to those who are bewildered and confused by that suffering. I can think of few things less helpful to someone going through pain than a sophisticated theological defence of the integrity of God, or even a gentle romp through the subtle logic of necessary evil.

Now that kind of discussion needs to take place. But it happens too often without any consideration of the anguish of those who need comforting and reassuring in the face of their sadness. Suffering is a pastoral and spiritual issue, not just a theological problem. In this book, I have not the slightest intention of presenting myself either as a spokesman or as some kind of defence attorney for God. God is perfectly capable of looking after himself. The real issue is not about defending God's honour or integrity, but about making sense of our experience. How can we relate God to our world of suffering? It is our grasp of the situation that is so often at fault, and needs to be explored. As I hope to show, taking the trouble to relate the depths of Christian thought to our experience of suffering can give us a fresh perspective which will transform and mature us.

For being a Christian does not mean avoiding suffering, as if God calls believers out of this world into a cosy Christian environment from which difficulties are banished. No. Believers are called to remain in the world, sharing its pain, and working to transform it from within. The cross of Christ stands as a solemn and powerful reminder that God himself was prepared to suffer in order to redeem his world, and that he expects his people to share the same commitment and pain as they share in the task of restoring a fallen world to its former glory. At the root of the Christian attitude to suffering is a passionate belief that our experience of suffering can, by the grace of God, be converted into something positive, which makes us better and more caring individuals and communities. Seen in the right manner, and offered to God for his most gentle healing touch, suffering can be transfigured into something glorious, which draws us closer to him and hints of that final time in the new Jerusalem when suffering will be nothing more than a memory.

2

BLAMING GOD

Many writers on the theme of suffering have turned to the writings of the great nineteenth-century Russian novelist Fyodor Dostoyevsky for inspiration. In his *The Brothers Karamazov*, Dostoyevsky tells of a harrowing incident in which an autocratic Russian ruler sets a pack of dogs upon an unfortunate child. They tear him to pieces. Ivan Karamazov, one of the central characters of the novel, registers a powerful protest against this action. He declares that he is going to hand God back his ticket.

As Karl Marx once wrote, 'the important thing is not to understand the world, but to change it'. If Marx is right, theories about suffering cut no ice – unless they allow us to abolish it. In a Marxist's eyes, Karamazov's protest is utterly futile. He may hand God back his ticket. Big deal! What does that accomplish? He makes some kind of moral statement, but does it stop suffering in the world?

When I was a teenager, I was strongly attracted to Marxism. Like many of my contemporaries, I saw it as the answer to society's suffering and injustice. I was an idealist, and, like many young people, I was entranced by ideals which I thought could be realised. Marxism appealed to that idealism, and fuelled it. It seemed to have the answer to suffering. Suffering was the result of the inhuman social conditions, faulty economics, and the political corruption of capitalism. Abolish capitalism, and the ills of the world would cease. When the revolution came, suffering would finally end, while a new era in the history of the human race dawned.

It was a profoundly attractive vision. I have no difficulty in understanding why I, and so many others, shared it, and eagerly looked forward to its fulfilment. Yet, it was only a dream. Like most forms of idealism, it was Utopian. In 1519, the English statesman and scholar Thomas More invented the word 'Utopia', to mean 'a non-existent paradise'. Human nature seems to need Utopias to keep it going, by giving it hope through an idealistic vision for the future. Marxism filled that need, for me and for many others.

I was like the American writer Lincoln Steffens, who visited the Soviet Union in 1919, two years after the Russian Revolution. 'I have been over into the future,' he declared, 'and it works.' But now the Soviet Union has gone the way of all Utopias, denounced and discredited by its inhabitants. So often, the attractiveness of a belief proves to be in inverse proportion to its truth. So often it seems that the more we want to believe in something, the less likely it is that this belief will rest upon truth. That is why it is so important for theology to reassure believers that the Christian hope is not Utopian, but real.

The recent experience of the Soviet Union and other militantly atheist states suggests that abandoning faith in God, far from liberating humanity from suffering, actually creates far more. Belief in God is a vital restraining factor. It curbs human evil by stressing God's condemnation of those who inflict suffering on others. Unless a belief system can actually eliminate suffering, its protests against God are nothing more than rhetoric; theoretical approaches to suffering are pointless unless they can change our situation. Unless atheism does something to get rid of pain and suffering, or the way in which we understand it, it has nothing to commend it.

Still, it would be wrong to accuse Marxism of being especially naive or misguided. Modern Western culture also fosters the illusion of being able to overcome suffering. We were informed that better education would eliminate the causes of suffering. Nothing of the sort has happened. We were confidently told that better medical care would alleviate human suffering. But the root causes of suffering remain, which the medical profession can at best reduce by skilled use of pain-killing drugs. In short, the Western liberal dream hoped that social evolution would lead to the elimination of human misery through the dawn of a brave new world. But paradise seems to have been postponed – yet again.

Many people seem unable to cope with this harsh reality. Instead of acknowledging that there seems to be something wrong with human nature, causing people to inflict suffering on others, they have taken the easy way out, blaming God for all the ills of the world. Many Jews became atheists as a result of the dreadful events that took place in the Second World War, especially in the extermination camps. But it wasn't God who engineered the holocaust. It was human beings. It wasn't God who developed the atom bomb, nor he who dropped it on Hiroshima. It wasn't God who directed the liquidation squads during Stalin's purges. It was sinful and fallen human beings. This dreadful truth shatters the shallow and facile optimism of liberalism, which insists in the most doctrinaire manner upon the basic goodness of humanity. Humanity's darker side is conveniently ignored. 'The scum and glory of the universe' was Pascal's judgement on human nature. Capable of soaring to tremendous artistic, cultural and moral heights, we are just as prone to sink to the most appalling depths. Trying to pin the blame on God is a crude evasion of human responsibility, which is as unfair as it is unrealistic.

A more helpful approach is to ask the following question. Why do we get so angry with God when people

suffer? Why are we so distressed when someone we love
suffers and dies?

Our sense of loss and sorrow when someone dies
is in direct proportion to how much we love them.
Our heartache would cease if we cared nothing for
anyone, and regarded everyone with a splendid sense
of detachment. Like the Stoics of old, we could then
remain unaffected by the suffering and death of those
around us. As a philosophy of life, this seems to have
much in its favour. The problem of suffering recedes
(unless, of course, we must suffer ourselves). But the
price paid is astonishingly high – too high for any
normal human being to take it seriously. Why? Because
it involves sacrificing one of the most basic aspects of
human nature – love and concern for others. There is
something about human nature which makes us want
to care for others, and to be cared for by them. Tennyson
hits the nail right on the head with some lines from 'In
Memoriam':

> 'Tis better to have loved and lost
> Than never to have loved at all.

We suffer when those whom we love suffer. Love is the
link which unites us with the lives of others, and allows
the pain of their suffering to spill over into our lives.
There is a bitter-sweet bond between love and suffering
– a bond which the cross itself, as we shall see, both
demonstrates and strengthens.

Jesus wept for his friend Lazarus. And those who
were witness to those tears realised what they meant.
'See how he loved him' (John 11:35–6). Love was what
united Christ and Lazarus, which moved the former to
tears on account of the plight of the latter. The gospel
demands that we should love one another, and bear one
another's burdens. Yet the more we love others, the
more we are moved and saddened by their suffering.

The command to love is a command to share in the sufferings of others.

This insight is vital to any responsible Christian approach to suffering. For just as we are moved by the sufferings of those whom we love, so God is moved by the pain and sorrow of those whom he loves. For the Christian, the extent of the love of God is not in doubt: the Son of God died in order that we might know its full depths. It is not as if God is unaffected by our suffering. Just as Christ wept over the dead Lazarus, so our compassionate God weeps alongside us as we mourn for our friends, suffer and die. The pages of history are stained by the tears of our God, who is working to bring about the day when 'There will be no more death or mourning or crying or pain' (Revelation 21:4).

But this naturally raises the following question: why doesn't God end suffering now?

3

GOD ALMIGHTY?

If God can do anything, why doesn't he put an end to suffering? If he is omnipotent, why can't he decree that suffering will be abolished with immediate effect? That sort of thought has gone through my mind many times. It is hardly an original thought. Just about everyone asks questions like that at some time in their lives. It is the familiarity, not the originality, of the question that obliges Christians to give some kind of answer.

The problem could be summed up like this. God is omnipotent. The meaning of that is simple. God can do anything he chooses to. Of course, we have to make allowance for the logicians, who, feeling piqued at being left out of most theological discussions, want to get a word in edgeways here. 'God can't make a square circle! He would contradict himself if he did.' The logic of this is undeniable. Squares and circles are both shapes. They are different shapes. So a single shape cannot be both a square and a circle. God could make a circle. He could make a square. But not a square circle. And thanking the logicians for their contribution, we may pass on. We may store this point in our memory, in the hope that it might, for once, be useful. But the real problem lies elsewhere.

The real problem is that we are not critical enough in our thinking about God. We tend to think we already know exactly what God is like. We don't need to be told anything about him. And so we happily begin our speculation. God can do anything. That makes a lot of sense. If he couldn't, he wouldn't be God, would he? But where does this idea actually come from? Let's ask a more difficult question. Does it fit in with a Christian understanding of God? In fact, it does not. We need to inquire very carefully about what Christianity actually says about God. By doing so we might well end up by upsetting the applecart of much popular thinking about lots of things – things such as the problem of suffering. So let's begin to explore our question with this point in mind.

Can God really do anything? Could he command someone to hate him, for example? A quick check suggests that there is no logical contradiction here. But there still seems to be something terribly wrong. Although there is no contradiction within the statement itself, it seems to fly in the face of everything we know about God. It is not logic, but basic Christianity, which is offended. The problem is not internal (with the logic), but external (with the view of God it implies). Let's try another example.

Could God prevent every human being that has ever turned to him in faith from being saved? A quick logical check suggests that all is well with this possibility. No square circles lurking in the background there. At the logical level, there is no difficulty in declaring that God, being omnipotent, could deny salvation to everyone that has ever trusted in him. But basic Christian faith is outraged. For deep down, we know that God just isn't like that. Scripture does not allow us to think of God in this way. The God that we know and love has promised in Scripture to save people who put their trust in him. If God were to deny them all salvation, he would contradict everything that we know about him; he would be breaking his promise. But the logician would immediately reply that there is no logical contradiction in breaking a promise. People do it all the time. What's the problem? Why should being all-powerful stop anyone from breaking promises? Being omnipotent is about power, not morality. There is a moral difficulty, admittedly. Logic, however, remains untainted by this potential lapse in divine fidelity. 'A fat lot of use logic is in theology!' might be an obvious retort. But this little skirmish into the realms of theological fancy has exposed an important and neglected aspect of the problem of suffering.

The simple fact of the matter is that God is not now able to do everything. His hands are tied. He has made promises – promises which limit his freedom of action. And he is faithful to those promises. And those promises are not arbitrary. They reflect and rest upon God's unchanging character. Those promises tell us about the way God is. They express his consistency and faithfulness, as well as offer us salvation. What God *promises* expresses what God *is*.

Some further exploration is in order. Let us try and imagine God in eternity, before the creation of the universe as we know it. What sort of options might he have had? Two obvious ones might be:

1 To create a universe.
2 Not to create a universe.

God is perfectly free to choose either of these possibilities. Now notice that they are mutually exclusive. Doing one means not doing the other. God cannot do them both – not because of any weakness or inability on his part, but simply because we are talking about an utter absurdity. The statement 'God can create the universe and at the same time not create the universe' is simply a meaningless combination of words, which does not suddenly make sense just because the word 'God' is slipped in at its beginning. (Maybe logic has its uses after all!)

But what happens when one of these possibilities is actualised? Suppose God were to decide to create a universe. As Christianity teaches, this decision rests on the nature of God himself. <u>It was not forced upon God, but was chosen by him, in accordance with his unchanging character.</u> It expresses his nature and purpose. So he duly brings a universe into being. Could he will this universe to cease to exist, simply because he had changed his mind?

No. God's decision to create a universe expresses the nature of God himself. It is not arbitrary or negotiable. God's decisions express God's nature. Furthermore, God's nature is unchanging. He is consistent in what he is, and thus in what he does. Once God acts, he is bound by his actions. He has made a decision. He has himself imposed limitations upon his freedom for action.

Again, consider two quite different possibilities open to God in eternity, before the founding of the world:

1 To offer salvation to all those who repent and turn to him.
2 To deny salvation to all those who repent and turn to him.

(Note that there is no logical difficulty with either of these options.)

The Bible affirms that God selected the first of these two options. Everything we know about God through Christ and in Scripture points unhesitatingly towards this fact. But could he change his mind? Could he now declare that the rules of the game have been changed, and that from this moment onwards, salvation will be withheld from all those who repent and turn to him?

<u>No. A promise rests upon the faithfulness of the one</u> who promises. It expresses both the *content* of that

promise (what is being offered to us) and the *trust-worthiness* of the one who offers it to us. God has promised to act in a certain way. He has established a definite process of salvation, which will apply until the end of history. He is faithful and reliable, and will not go back on the promises sealed and declared in his Son, Jesus Christ.

God is faithful and reliable. And for that very reason, he cannot be omnipotent. This might seem a strange thing to suggest. However, a little reflection will bring out the vital point. To be reliable means that you do not – and more than that, that you cannot – break a promise. It means that you cannot arbitrarily change your mind. Take two statements like this:

1 God can change his mind about things, and need not be restricted by what he promised in the past.
2 God is faithful to his promises.

At the logical level, these statements are both perfectly acceptable. But the logician will immediately add a vital point: they cannot both be true at the same time. If the first is true, the second is false – and vice versa. The theologian will then insist that it is the second which is true. And thus God cannot do anything; his options are restricted, because he has chosen to restrict them.

Now if you are omnipotent, you can do what you like. If God is totally omnipotent, then no options are closed off to him, except those which are logically impossible. But the simple fact is that the God whom Christians know and worship, and who makes himself known in and through Jesus Christ, is steadfast, constant and faithful.

The great theologians of the later Middle Ages, such as William of Ockham, were perfectly familiar with the point at issue. In his famous discussion of the opening line of the Apostle's Creed – 'I believe in God the

Father almighty' – Ockham moves in immediately to
ask precisely what is meant by that deceptively simple
word 'almighty'. It cannot, he argues, mean that God is
presently able to do everything, although it does mean
that God was *once* free to act in this way. God has
established an order of things which reflects his loving
and righteous will – and that order, once established,
will remain until the end of time.

Ockham uses two terms to refer to these different
options. The *absolute power of God* refers to God's options before he had committed himself to any course of
action or world ordering. The *ordained power of God*
refers to the way things are, which reflects the will of
God their creator. These do not represent two different
sets of options now open to God. They represent two
different moments in the history of human salvation.
And our concern is with the ordained power of God, the
way in which God orders his creation at present.

For Ockham, God cannot now do everything. He
has deliberately limited his possibilities. In his omnipotence, God chose to limit his own options. Is that a
contradiction? No. If God is really capable of doing
anything, he must be able to commit himself to a
course of action – and stay committed to it. Otherwise,
there is something which God cannot do, thus calling
into question his omnipotence. Ockham's approach,
though long neglected, needs to be recovered and
valued; for it represents a responsible, helpful and
thoroughly Christian approach to the question of God's
omnipotence.

Another way of thinking focuses on the idea of the
covenant between God and his people. God entered into
a covenant with his people, by which he swore to be
their God. ' "This is the covenant that I will make
with the house of Israel after that time," declares the
Lord. "I will put my law in their minds and write it on
their hearts. I will be their God, and they will be my

people"' (Jeremiah 31:33). This represents a promise and a commitment. Can God now break this promise? Can he renege on this commitment? No. That would involve God behaving in a way inconsistent with his very nature. Having promised, God keeps his word. His options are limited by his promises on the one hand, and his faithful nature on the other. He is no longer able to do *everything*.

So where does this leave all the abstract talk about God being omnipotent? In something of a state of ruin, is the short answer. The neat simplifications of the philosophers are left in tatters. God is indeed almighty. But that does not mean that he can do anything and everything. His choices are limited. This limitation does not arise from any weakness or failure upon the part of God, but from a decision to deliberately restrict his own options. It is a self-imposed limitation, not something that is imposed upon God. Only God had the right and the ability to limit his own course of action.

So what bearing do these thoughts have on human suffering? First, let us note the way in which God is affected by suffering. A totally omnipotent god could have avoided being affected in any way by the sorrow and grief of the world. But 'the God of the Christians' (Tertullian) – the God that we are talking about – *is* pained by the suffering of the world. His very nature leads him to decide that he will enter into it, as one of us, in the person of his Son, Jesus Christ. In his love for us, he bears our sorrows and is acquainted with our grief. God allowed himself to be hurt by the suffering of the world.

We need to let this point sink in. God decided to be hurt by our pain. God allowed himself to suffer as we suffer and to share in our grief. Just as Jesus wept over the tomb of his dead friend Lazarus, so God is moved by our sadness. The cross is the supreme demonstration of God's solidarity with us in this world of suffering. He *chose* to enter this world, he *chose* to share its sorrow and pain, and he *chose* finally to suffer death on a cross. Not because he had to, as if he was under some kind of external pressure to do so – but because he wanted to.

4

A LOVING GOD?

If God is so loving, why does he allow suffering? The fact of suffering calls into question the goodness of God. Suffering and love seem to many to be mutually exclusive. The argument leading to this conclusion is usually set out like this:

1 God is almighty.
2 God is completely loving.
3 There is suffering and evil in the world.

As things stand, however, there is no inconsistency – yet. A fourth idea has to be added before there is a logical problem. There is a logical contradiction if either,

1 An almighty and loving God could eliminate suffering entirely,

or,

2 There are no good reasons for God to allow suffering.

If either or both of these could be shown to be right, a serious problem with the Christian view of God might well have been exposed. But they have not been shown to be true.

The believer, having been asked some hard questions by the critics of Christianity, now has a right to ask some equally hard questions in reply. How do they know that there cannot be good reasons for God permitting

suffering? Pain serves a vital biological function –
that of alerting us to injury, and the need for treat-
ment. It serves to warn us of danger. <u>And suffering
serves a vital spiritual function. It reminds us of our
mortality, preventing us from entertaining delusions
about our nature and our future</u>.

But some would reply that a world in which there
is suffering cannot be a good world. Surely God could
have created a better world? If this is the kind of
world that God created, he can't be up to much. All
too often, this argument proves to be purely rhetorical.
<u>These critics are putting themselves in the position
of declaring that they know a better world than that
which we know, must be possible.</u> Yet this approach
was devastatingly criticised by David Hume in the
eighteenth century. Writing against those who claimed
that this world was 'the best of all possible worlds',
Hume stressed that we know only this world. We have
nothing else to compare it with. We have no absolutely
valid reasons for suggesting either that this is the
best of all possible worlds – or indeed, that it is *not*
the best of all possible worlds.

The real problem does not lie at the level of logic,
but in our intuitive feeling that a loving God could
not allow suffering. <u>Somehow, we seem to imagine
that suffering is the direct opposite of love, so that
the Christian belief in 'a loving God' is inconsistent
with the presence of suffering in the world.</u> Yet in
reality love and suffering are not necessarily opposed
at all. <u>Indeed, they often stand together, almost as if
they were two sides of the same coin.</u> I have always
thought that one of the chief glories of the Christian
faith is the way in which it links love and suffering.
<u>How is the love of God shown? Supremely through the
suffering and death of Jesus Christ.</u>

The suffering of the Son of God is the most urgent
and persuasive demonstration of the amazing extent

to which God loves us. Where some suggest that love
should abolish suffering, or that love can only be expressed in a world without pain, the gospel knows of
a love that makes itself known in and through the
suffering of Christ. That insight seems to me to be
not merely astonishing; it holds the key to new ways
of coping with the grim reality of suffering. The ancient
Stoics taught us to suffer with dignity; Christ allows us
to suffer in hope.

But how can suffering and love co-exist in God? An
objection might go like this. 'If God is really loving, he
would want us all to be happy. But we suffer. And we
are not happy when we suffer. Therefore God cannot be
loving.' But what sort of idea of happiness is involved
here? What sort of happiness are we meant to pursue?
The idea of 'happiness' is all too often used in a trivial
way, as if the individual were the centre and measure
of all things. If I were phenomenally wealthy, I would
be happy. Or would I? Would I not sleep uneasily,
beset by a whole new range of problems, moral and
practical, arising from the possession of wealth? How
would I keep it? I might be a target for kidnappers,
extortionists, and the tax authorities. And what of
those others who are poor in order that I can be rich? I
might well dream of a paradise in which I was totally
happy, with all my needs and cares being taken care
of by others. But what of those others?

What of the slaves who made the planters of the
Deep South happy? What of the underpaid and under-
nourished workers of the third world, who provide the
goods that make me cosy and happy? What is the cost
of my self-centred and happy world? My happiness
is purchased through the suffering of others. Paradoxically, it is only by studiously ignoring the social
cost of individual happiness that I can maintain that
illusion of happiness. Being aware of the price paid for
this personal gratification ought to make us develop a

social conscience which willingly sacrifices individual happiness in order to promote the common good.

So could we really believe in a god who just pampers individuals, making them 'happy'? And can we really equate 'love' with 'making us feel good'? Only 'love' in the shallowest sense of the word would content itself with indulging the appetites, ambitions and vices of individual humans. But this is not what the love of God is like. We must do God the basic justice of allowing *his* idea of love to be heard. Too often, we rush into discussions of 'love and suffering' on the basis of our assumption that we already know exactly what love means. But we need to be taught what love, in the fully Christian sense of the word, actually means. We do not know; we need to learn.

The love of God is not some kind of indulgent benevolence which smiles upon our whims without asking whether they are innocent or profoundly destructive, and then generously allows us to have what we want. It involves our transformation. It involves our reshaping, so that we may desire and receive those things which are, in the mind of God our creator, for our greatest good. God has created us; we must listen to our maker concerning what is best for us. Precisely because of God's astonishing and overwhelming love for us, shown through the death of Christ upon the cross, he wants us to have nothing but the best. And what could be better than fellowship with God – something which nothing can ever destroy? George Herbert makes this point superbly in his poem 'Love'.

> Love bade me welcome; yet my soul drew back,
>   Guilty of dust and sin.
> But quick-eyed Love, observing me grow slack
>   From my first entrance in,
> Drew nearer to me, sweetly questioning
>   If I lacked anything.

'A guest,' I answered, 'worthy to be here.'
> Love said, 'You shall be he.'
'I, the unkind, ungrateful? Ah, my dear,
> I cannot look on thee.'
Love took my hand, and smiling did reply,
> 'Who made the eyes but I?'

'Truth, Lord, but I have marred them; let my shame
> Go where it doth deserve.'
'And know you not', says Love, 'who bore the
> blame?'
> 'My dear, then I will serve.'
'You must sit down', says Love, 'and taste my meat.'
> So I did sit and eat.

But this, some will object, is pure paternalism, even if it is also splendid poetry. It is absurd to look to God to tell us what is best for us. It is even more absurd to suggest that God himself meets all our needs and hopes. That is simply childish nonsense in an age in which humanity has grown up. Initially, this objection might seem to have some weight. But not for long. A survey of the monuments to recent major human decisions concerning what is best for our race hardly makes inspiring reading. The First World War; the gas chambers of Auschwitz; the atom bomb of Hiroshima; the killing fields of Cambodia. The list goes on. It is a terrifying monument to what happens when humans start acting as if they are God. It testifies to the unreliability of human notions of what is right. Hitler thought he knew what was best for the German people. That vision happened to involve the extermination of millions of people. Stalin had no doubts about what was best for the Soviet Union. That vision happened to involve the liquidation of anyone foolish enough to oppose him. Do we *really* have any idea of what is best for us? Are we *really* in a position to declare that we know, better than God, what is good for us?

But at the theological level, a far more profound argument comes into play. It is God who created us, not we ourselves. Can we really pretend that anyone other than our creator knows what is best for us? Can we really hope to stand in the place of God, and gain reliable insights into our origins, our present situation, and our future goal?

To go back to the images introduced earlier, we are on the Road, and need to be able to climb to the Balcony. In order to know what is right for us, we need to know where we are going. We need dependable knowledge of what our future is meant to hold for us, in order that we can move towards achieving that goal. But what is the future goal of humanity? For what purpose were we created? It is here that we need to attend to God.

The true goal of humanity is to be united (perhaps we should say, reunited?) to God. We have been created in the image of God, with the ultimate aim of finding our rest in him. The love of God is concerned with enabling us to achieve our true and God-given potential – that is, to find peace and fulfilment with the living and loving God. Yet through sin, we have a natural tendency to desire things that are ruinous and inappropriate – perhaps without realising that they are so. Augustine of Hippo, perhaps one of the wisest critics of naive notions of human goodness, made this point with his famous analogy of a pair of scales.

Some, he suggested, saw the human will as being like a pair of perfectly balanced scales. Right and wrong, good and evil, can thus be weighed up in the respective scale pans, and a balanced judgement reached. But what, Augustine asked, of sin? What of the corruption of human nature? The situation was actually quite different. The human will is like a pair of scales, one of whose pans is loaded. There is a perceptible bias towards evil. It may vary from one person to another

– but it is there. Left to its own devices, we will tend to choose the visible over the invisible, and the creation over the creator. As a result, the human will often find it difficult to desire what is right, let alone achieve it.

'Love', in the trivial, human sense of the term would not merely respect this situation; it would pamper it, by indulging the desires which arise from it. But this cannot be allowed to pass for the love of God. The love of God wishes to transform our situation, to liberate us from the tyranny of sin, and to allow us to desire and receive those things which are best for us. We must be liberated from our infatuation with things which threaten to prevent us from achieving our purpose and finding our goal.

The great prize which is set before us is none other than a relationship with God himself. But our vision is so distorted by sin that we see nothing but the lesser prizes around us. We are called by God to find our rest in him. But our hearing is so dulled that we hear only the voices of the world and its transient goals. We settle for the shadows of the grand delights for which we were created. So powerful is the hold of sin upon us that we have lowered our sights, fixing them upon the creation rather than the creator. And so love, in the full and Christian sense of the term, must free us from this mess. Sin, like a swamp, bogs us down, preventing us from breaking free. So how can we be liberated?

The first step towards freedom is invariably taken only after we realise that we are imprisoned. If we are to long for liberation, we must realise that we are in bondage. Love must therefore tell us that we are lost, before it can delight us with the declaration that we have been found. We, who think we know it all, and know it best, must be brought to our senses. The re-assuring set of beliefs that we have woven around our-selves like a cocoon must be unravelled. Death need not be feared if we overlook its existence, or believe that

it happens only to others. God is obliged to bring about
the funeral of a great myth – the myth of our personal
immortality and the permanence of the world. These
things must pass, and we shall pass with them. But
God will live on – and so can we, in union with him. But
not if we cling steadfastly to the world and its values.

Suffering and the death of those we know and love
break down the pretence of human permanence. We
do not want to admit our own mortality. We find it
deeply threatening to accept that the world and all
whom we love will one day pass beyond our grasp. It
is so much more reassuring to believe that we and the
world will go on for ever – that we will be able to hold
on to all the glittering prizes which we win during
life. But the reality is very different. Suffering strips
away our illusions of immortality. It causes anxiety to
rear its ugly, yet revealing, head. It batters down the
gates of the citadel of illusions. It confronts us with
the harsh facts of life. And it makes us ask those
hard questions which have the power to erode false-
hood and propel us away from the false security and
transient rewards of the world towards our loving God.

'Funerals,' a colleague once remarked to me, 'are
intended to remind those present that they are still
alive – for the time being.' Hospitals are powerful
symbols of human frailty and mortality, tokens of our
vulnerability. Think of sin as a force, a power which
opposes our coming home to God. It is like gravity,
pulling things down. Our innate human inertia, made
worse by sin, encourages us to remain within our com-
fortable view of the world, and not to inquire too deeply
about its foundations. It is easier to close our eyes to
the signs of loss, parting and transience which surround
us, and threaten to undermine our cosy assumptions. If
eternity intersects our history at any point, it is at those
moments when we realise that we, like all of humanity,
are ephemeral creatures whose lot, if limited to the

world of the senses, must indeed be an unhappy one.

Yet it need not be. Our eyes need to be lifted to catch a glimpse of another country; to hear its music. We are tied to this earth by sin, like gravity; something needs to be done to break its hold. Suffering, though tragic, is not pointless. It is the pin which bursts the balloon of our delusions, and opens the way to an urgent and passionate wrestling with the reality of death and the question of what lies beyond. It is only by breaking the surly bonds which shackle us to this dying world that we can reach out and embrace the greatest and finest prize we can ever attain – being enfolded in the love of God.

There is an irony here. Love is active in something which appears to deny love. The passionate care of God for his creatures shines through something which seems to deny that care, just as the light of the sun pierces through clouds. Perhaps the finest discussion of this point is by Martin Luther, who made the suffering of Christ and his people the centrepiece of his 'theology of the cross'. How, Luther asked, could a loving God tolerate suffering? His answer takes the following form.

All Christian thought about the nature and purposes of God must be grounded in the cross of Christ. It is here that true theology and the knowledge of God are to be found. The cross puts everything to the test. In the words of Nicholas Ridley, who was martyred on 16th October 1555, '*coticula fidei crux*, the cross is the touchstone of faith'. The love of God, Luther stresses, is revealed through the suffering of Christ, not despite that suffering. The Christian church came into being through that suffering, and shall share in that suffering, before finally sharing in the glory of the risen Christ.

Luther then draws a central distinction. Sometimes, God works in a way which is obviously consistent with his nature – a way of action which Luther terms '*opus*

proprium Dei, the proper work of God'. But at other
times, God works in a way which initially seems to
contradict his nature, yet on further reflection is seen
to be totally consistent with it. Luther refers to this as
'*opus alienum Dei*, the strange work of God'. As an example, he suggests we think about God's condemnation
of sinners. Initially, this seems to contradict what we
know of God. Is not God merciful and compassionate?

But then we realise how superficial this idea of God
is. It treats God as sickly sweet and sentimental, and
ignores the whole question of our sin and his righteousness. Knowing that we are condemned alerts us
to the reality of our situation – that we are sinners,
that we stand under the wrath of God, that we seem
to have no claim whatsoever to mercy and forgiveness. And so we turn in our hopelessness to God.
We abandon our pretensions of adequacy, and learn
of his mercy and grace; we repent of our sin and
receive forgiveness and mercy. So something which
initially seems to contradict God's compassion turns
out to be consistent with it. God uses means which
seem to be out of line with his nature in order to bring
about a goal which is obviously true to his nature.

Think of suffering as 'the strange work of God'. It
is not an end in itself, but a means to a greater end
– that of bringing us home to God, where suffering is
transfigured and eventually defeated. Just as Christ
defeated death by his own death, so human suffering proves to hold the key to its own eventual transformation. The proper work of God is our salvation;
suffering allows God to achieve that end. Far from
being an utter absurdity, by the grace of God suffering is able to serve a purpose.

Luther asks that we take suffering seriously, and
learn why it is the cross – the symbol of suffering –
which stands at the centre of our faith. Perhaps more
than any other Christian writer, he acknowledges its

reality – the reality and pain of the suffering of Christ on the cross, and of believers as they share in that suffering. The Christian Church is an extension of the passion of Christ. We are called to be members of the suffering people of God. But Luther also asks that we see beyond suffering; that we do not limit the power and presence of God to what we experience. The resurrection reminds us that, despite all appearances, God was indeed a hidden participant at Calvary. Just as those present at the crucifixion failed to recognise that God was present at that dreadful scene, let alone that he was able to work something positive through it, so we fail to realise that God can be present in human suffering, and able to transfigure it.

5

DISSATISFACTION WITH THE WORLD

'Man is the only animal that laughs and weeps; for he is the only animal that is struck by the difference between what things are and what they might have been' (William Hazlitt). Many people are profoundly dissatisfied with this world. Deep down within them, they sense that there must be something better somewhere. Now these feelings are real and important, and they serve a vitally important function. Our natural instinct is to protest, and shout out 'Why can't the world be better? Because it's not better, we don't want to believe in God!'

But then theology asks for a hearing. First, it points out that we are judging the reality against an ideal. Dissatisfaction with our present situation does not necessarily imply that a better alternative exists! It is like comparing our own lives with those lived by a story-book prince, or a fairy-tale princess. This ideal might be like the dreams of fairy tales – a pleasant fiction, and nothing more. It might provoke a sense of wistful longing for a happier land – but that is no guarantee that such a land exists. We have to ask hard questions about this sense of dissatisfaction. Why do we possess such a deep-seated sense that things could be better than this? Where does this sense come from?

An important answer is provided by a distinguished group of Christian writers, from Augustine to Milton, who argued that the profound sense of dissatisfaction with many aspects of the world as we know it is to be explained as a nostalgia, a sense of longing for a lost Eden, a wish to return to a land in which suffering and death did not exist. And this memory of Eden is also an anticipation of the heavenly Jerusalem, in which suffering and death will once more cease to exist, as the 'bliss of Eden' (Milton) is restored.

Our sense of dissatisfaction is thus a memory of this haunting 'bliss of Eden'. It arises from a yearning for the innocence of the first days of creation, which will one day be restored through the process of redemption in Christ. And so this sense of dissatisfaction is also prophetic. It points ahead to the fulfilment of the Christian hope in the world to come. There must be a better world than this – and that will come to pass in the heavenly Jerusalem. And it is at this point that the Christian hope begins to make its presence felt. For the gospel declares that, one day, such a world will exist. It insists that the world we now know will be replaced by a new heaven and a new earth. This sense of dissatisfaction is God-given, intended to remind us that this world is not our home. It is intended to make us yearn for the world which is to come.

Naturally, this will not satisfy the armchair critics of God, who will promptly declare that *they* could have created a universe devoid of any suffering and pain. But could they really? Sadly (for we would like to believe them), this invariably turns out to be the rhetoric of dissatisfaction, which promises a better world as a matter of principle, rather than of fact. These people would promise us anything, if it increased our dissatisfaction with our present situation. The idea of a pain-free world is just about as Utopian a delusion as you can find anywhere. A world without suffering would be a world without life as we know it. Suffering is the price we pay for living. And though that price tag is expensive, it is something that most are willing to pay.

And secondly, theology reminds us that this is a fallen world – a world which has been ruined by sin, and which will one day be restored. And it assures us that our feelings of dissatisfaction are genuine and important, because they give birth to the hope of a new earth and a new heaven, in which suffering and pain will be a thing of the past.

Theology makes sense of this feeling of longing for an ideal world in which there is no suffering. Suffering is like a gadfly, continually irritating us, provoking us to ask hard questions. How can the suffering of this world be alleviated? When will this world become a better place? And it is not just Christians who have wrestled with this question. Let us explore a secular option, now widely discredited, before returning to the Christian approach.

One of the most important – and, until recently, one of the most influential – secular answers to this question was provided by Karl Marx. The Marxist analysis of human experience recognises this feeling of dissatisfaction with the way the world is, and claims the ability to cure it. Come the revolution, this sense of dissatisfaction (which is a direct result of capitalism) will disappear. But in those parts of the world where the revolution came, this sense of dissatisfaction obstinately remained. The revolution failed to get rid of suffering. Pain, and all the questions which its presence raises, remained unanswered and unresolved. Marxism, like other secular answers to the riddle of suffering, failed to satisfy.

The New Testament also promises the ending of suffering. The sufferings of the present age can only be ended through the final coming of the kingdom of God (Romans 8:18–25). The present sufferings are like birth-pangs – suffering which anticipates the coming of new life. This coming of the kingdom will one day happen to every believer, through their death, their bodily resurrection, and their joyful entry into eternal life in the New Jerusalem. It is this hope which keeps Christian believers going in life. Indeed, it is our anticipation of the life of the New Jerusalem, in which suffering is ended and tears are wiped away, that makes us so dissatisfied with the world as we now know it. We are restless in the world, and long to find our rest in the New Jerusalem.

One of the finest expressions of this feeling, and its most exquisite theological interpretation, may be found in the famous words of Augustine of Hippo: 'You have made us for yourself, and our hearts are restless until they rest in you.' Throughout Augustine's reflections, especially in the *Confessions*, the same theme recurs. We are doomed to remain incomplete in our present existence.

There is a sense of postponement, of longing, of wistful yearning, of groaning under the strain of having to tolerate the sufferings of the present, when the future offers so much. Perhaps the finest statement of this exquisite agony is found in Augustine's cry that he 'is groaning with inexpressible groaning in my distant wandering, and remembering Jerusalem with my heart stretching upwards in longing for it, Jerusalem my fatherland, Jerusalem my mother.'

Theology, then, acknowledges the reality of our distress at the presence of suffering in the world. But it has things to say that we need to hear. Christians feel the pain of suffering so intensely on account of the vision of the creation as it will be on that day when suffering ends and human tears are wiped dry for the last time. Why can it not happen sooner? Why does God not end the present order now? Why wait?

And it is on precisely this note that the Revelation of St John ends. Having glimpsed the joy of the New Jerusalem, and tasted the peace of the new heaven and the new earth, John cannot bear to wait any longer.

'Come, Lord Jesus,' he cries (Revelation 22:20). And we share his feelings, as we survey the sadness and sorrow of the world.

Much the same feelings are expressed in Paul's letter to the Christians at Philippi, in which the apostle finds himself torn between the joy of going to be with Christ, and the work that remains for him on earth. 'For to me, to live is Christ and to die is gain . . . I am torn between the two: I desire to depart and be with Christ, which is better by far; but it is more necessary for you that I remain in the body' (Philippians 1:21–4).

Suffering makes us yearn to be with Christ, in the heavenly realms. It strengthens and nourishes our hope, and thus makes us impatient with the way things are – of which suffering is a symptom. But as the example of Jesus Christ reminds us, resurrection lies on the far side of suffering. That hope is enough to keep us going in the face of suffering – and to make us want to share that hope with others who suffer without faith.

6

SUFFERING AND THE GOD OF THE PHILOSOPHERS

Since history began, the existence of pain, suffering and evil in the world have been recognised. Christian theology has learned to live with the reality of pain and evil. It is not as if suffering were a well-kept secret, the existence of which has suddenly been sprung upon a world which fervently believed it did not exist.

Yet some would have us believe that suffering *is* something new. The last hundred years have seen new horrors of suffering, through wars of unparalleled destructiveness and viciousness, through the deliberate causation of famine (such as that which Stalin inflicted upon the Ukraine), and through the ruthless exploitation of the environment and of ethnic minorities. For reasons such as this, we are told that God cannot be taken seriously any more.

But why should we accept this reckless assertion? Human sinfulness has caused untold human suffering. The great liberal vision of moral progress through the harnessing of technology and the sciences has collapsed. The technology which was meant to alleviate suffering has been used to cause pain and death. The sciences have been remorselessly exploited to develop new and more efficient ways to eliminate unwanted human beings. It is not the idea of God, but a doctrinaire belief in the goodness of human nature, which has been shattered by the sufferings of the present age. And if that is a hard lesson to learn, it is nevertheless a lesson which *needs* to be learned.

Suffering is nothing new. What *is* new is a deeper intensity of pain and cruelty, brought about largely by human agency. An important historical fact should be noted here. Christian writers before the seventeenth century did not believe that suffering posed any serious threat to Christian belief. Indeed, I spent many years working through most of the major works on Christian theology written between the twelfth and sixteenth centuries, and cannot recall any of them treating the reality of suffering as a serious obstacle to Christian faith.

But the situation has changed. Why? Why is suffering seen as a challenge to faith, as never before? The answer lies in a dramatic development which took place during the seventeenth century, and which, according to many scholars, lies at the roots of modern atheism. Anxious to make Christianity intellectually respectable, a number of writers – such as Leonard Lessius and Marin Mersenne – argued that the best defence of the gospel was provided by philosophy. To defend the Christian faith, it was advisable to set aside traditional ways of justifying it, and instead to rely upon the wisdom of philosophy.

And so, instead of concentrating upon the significance of Jesus Christ for the question of whether God exists, and what he is like, an appeal should be made directly and exclusively to reason. Instead of an appeal to the Christian experience of the Holy Spirit, an appeal was to be made to nature. Reason and nature were thus the testing grounds on which the credibility of Christianity was to be judged. The end result was inevitable. Under the influence of these well-meaning but misguided people, Christianity entered into the defence of the existence of the Christian God without being able to appeal to anything recognisably or distinctly Christian. The resources that had served the gospel for century after century were squandered, discarded as relics of a past era.

Things went from bad to worse through the impact of the seventeenth-century philosopher René Descartes, who thought he had invented a neat and watertight defence of his faith. Under the influence of Descartes, this approach to the defence of Christianity would prove to have devastating results. Descartes argued that God was a totally perfect being, and developed a number of interesting philosophical arguments for the existence of God on the basis of this assumption. He seems to have thought that they raised Christianity to new heights of intellectual respectability.

In fact, they did nothing of the sort. The enormous emphasis which came to be placed upon the perfection of God by Descartes was totally compromised by the undeniable fact of the existence of evil and suffering. How could a perfect being allow such imperfection to exist? Descartes' 'god' is not the God of Christianity; it is simply a philosophical idea. His defence of Christianity is actually nothing of the sort; it is just a defence of an idea about God that Descartes happened to develop.

There is a story here that is worth retelling. France has produced many outstanding philosophers, scientists and mathematicians. Blaise Pascal may be numbered among the greatest of these. But he was also profoundly aware of the limitations of philosophical ways of thinking about God. The God of the Bible was intensely personal; Pascal believed passionately that philosophy had thrown away this insight.

After his death, his colleagues found a crumpled piece of paper sewed up inside his shirt. It was obviously so important to him that he wanted to carry it with him everywhere he went, pressed close to his heart. The words on this piece of paper have become legendary; they are intensely relevant to our theme. 'God of Abraham, God of Isaac, God of Jacob, not of philosophers and scholars, God of Jesus Christ, my

God and your God. Your God shall be my God.' Here
is a perceptive personal declaration of faith, and an
emphatic rejection of mere *ideas* of God in favour of
the personal reality of God in people's lives.

Now there is nothing wrong with philosophy. Philosophy makes us ask hard questions about how we
know anything. It forces us to think about our words
and ideas, and to make sure we know what we are doing
when we use them. The problems start to develop when
some philosophers argue that human reason itself can
tell us exactly what God is like. The 'god of the philosophers' is the product of a human reason which seems
to overlook the fact that God has taken the trouble to
tell us what he is like.

The 'god of the philosophers' is basically little more
than a perfect, ideal and abstract being, constructed
out of the distilled elements of human benevolence.
The characteristics of this god are primarily its omnipotence, omniscience and goodness. Its credibility – but
not that of the 'God and Father of our Lord Jesus
Christ' (1 Peter 1:3) – is instantly compromised by
suffering. As Alasdair MacIntyre, one of the most perceptive of modern philosophers, remarks, 'the God in
whom the nineteenth and twentieth centuries came to
disbelieve had been invented only in the seventeenth
century.' The god of philosophical theology is a human
invention, a product of human reason. Yet the God
to whom Christian faith and theology respond is a
living and loving being, who makes himself known to
us through Christ, Scripture and personal experience
– including, as we shall see, suffering.

As Pascal so clearly saw, the philosophical idea of
God bears little relation to the God of Jesus Christ –
our God. Somehow, the philosophical idea of God seems
bleak and dreary, both in itself and in comparison with
the joyful Christian experience of God. It reminds me of
Edwards' celebrated remarks to Samuel Johnson: 'You

are a philosopher, Dr Johnson. I have tried too in my time to be a philosopher, but I don't know how, cheerfulness was always breaking in.' The theologian, steeped in the knowledge of the resurrection of the suffering and crucified Christ, brings a certain sense of joy to the question of suffering – a joy which is conspicuously absent from the philosophical discussion of the question.

And what of the moral side of things? Descartes' god, like Aristotle's 'Unmoved Mover', stands immune from the sorrow of the world. It is uninvolved and detached, standing callously to one side while the world suffers. Like a Victorian lord of the manor enjoying a sumptuous lifestyle while remaining supremely indifferent to the deprivation and poverty of the lower classes, the god of Descartes is an offence and a scandal. It does not share in the pain and poverty of its people. Small wonder that there was a clamour for its abolition.

But the God and Father of our Lord Jesus Christ is very different. Here is no unmoved mover. Here is the creator of the world, who chose to enter into the pain, sorrow and sadness of the fallen world in order to restore it to its wholeness. Here is a God who knows pain at first hand, who shares the woes of his people. No longer can we speak about suffering alone and unnoticed. The experience of suffering has been taken up into the life of God.

There is much more that could be said on this point, and we shall reflect further upon it presently. But the main argument is clear: the God of Christianity and the god of Descartes are different. The death of the latter (which, as we stressed, is a relatively recent invention) need be the cause of little mourning. Christians now need to ensure that the world learns of the divine care and compassion made known through the passion and death of Jesus Christ.

So important is this point about the suffering of God that we must explore it further.

7

WHAT WAS GOD DOING ON THE CROSS?

The cross. Those two words sum up the greatest story that the world has ever been told. It is hard to read that story without being deeply moved. The majestic and dignified suffering of Jesus often moves people to ask deep questions about the cross. Why did this wonderful person have to suffer in this way? What was *God* doing on the cross? That's the question we're going to explore right now.

The first answer to that question might, at first sight, seem a little trivial. *He was there.* The man dying on the cross is no ordinary human being. Three men were crucified at Calvary. But there was something very different about the man on that central cross. He was content to be 'numbered with the transgressors' (Isaiah 53:12) – but he was not among their number. The meaning of the cross can only be grasped if we realise the identity of Jesus himself. As the resurrection made clear (Romans 1:3–4), the Son of God himself was nailed to that cruel cross; it was the Son of God who died on that cross, in order that we might live (John 3:16). Yet Jesus cried out 'My God, my God, why have you forsaken me?' (Mark 15:34). Sin cuts us off from God. Here we can see Christ taking the full weight of human sin, and all its consequences, on his lonely shoulders. In this moment of agony, Christ shares our sense of being cut off from God. In this great moment of humility, the burden of human sin was taken away from people

44

like ourselves, and laid upon Christ, who willingly and obediently 'bore the sin of many' (Isaiah 53:12).

Now it may not seem very important to begin by stressing that God really was there at Calvary. But it matters a lot – especially in relation to human suffering. For it tells us that God knows what it is like to suffer. The famous saying about the medical profession, 'Only the wounded physician can heal', highlights the fact that we are able to relate better to someone who has shared our problem, who has been through already what we are going through now – and has triumphed over it. In turning to God, we turn to one who knows and understands. Christ is the wounded physician of Calvary, one who shares our hurt and injury, and is able to comfort as he heals.

One of my favourite works of art is the famous Isenheim altarpiece by Matthias Grünewald. It portrays Christ on the cross, wounded and in great pain. By his feet are two people. On one side of the cross is Mary, who weeps for the loss of her son – a theme which inspired one of the greatest poems of all to meditate on the death of Christ, *Stabat Mater dolorosa*. On the other side is John the Baptist, extending his long arm as he points to the dying Christ. It is as if he is pointing away from himself towards Christ, the one he came as a herald to proclaim. He seems to be saying: '*This* is the one upon whom our faith rests in its totality. *This* is the man who holds the key to suffering and pain.' And yet there is another witness to the tragedy of that first Good Friday. Unseen and unportrayed is God himself, who suffers the loss of his only Son. We are reminded of the cost of redemption, of the pain endured by God in order that sin may be defeated, and of his love for us. That love is revealed through the suffering and death of Christ, as the Son of God endures all the grief, pain and affliction of human life for us.

From the perspective of the Road, Jesus Christ may seem like a fellow-traveller, someone who shares our journey along that difficult and winding way we call 'the life of faith'. But from the Balcony, he is seen to be very different from all of us. Here is God – the same God who made the heaven and the earth – who has chosen to spend time on the Road. Our place is on that Road; he chose to join us. He didn't have to; he wanted to. And his presence on that Road changes everything. Not only can we journey knowing that we are in the best of company; we also have new confidence in the reliability of that road, and are reassured of the certainty of reaching its final destination.

We are not dealing with a distant God who knows nothing of what being human, frail and mortal means. He knows and understands. So we can 'approach the throne of grace with confidence' (Hebrews 4:16).

It matters – it matters enormously – to know that God was present at Calvary. The cross tells us that God has been through the dark side of life, its pain and suffering. And so when we experience the darker side of life, we can turn to him in prayer, and in confidence that he knows what we are going through. It makes prayer at times of sadness and suffering so much more meaningful and real – as it is meant to be.

Christian theology uses the word 'incarnation' when it talks about Jesus becoming a human being. To talk about the incarnation, or about 'God incarnate', is to declare that God became one of us in Jesus Christ. If Jesus *is* God, then the sight of Jesus on the cross offers us many amazing insights about God, each of them worthy of a book in itself. Two of these insights may be considered, before we move on.

First, if Jesus is God, then he is the best visual aid for God the world has ever known. We all know how difficult it can be to speak about God at times, partly because we find it hard to picture him. Very often

'God' is little more than an abstract idea. Now, God has authorised us to think of Jesus when we try to think about him. To have seen Jesus is to have seen the Father. Jesus is a window into God.

Try to imagine that you are talking to someone about the character of God. You want to explain to them how awesome his love is. Without Jesus, you might find yourself faltering a little, as you grasp for words to try and explain the wonder of that love. You might wander from one cliché to another: 'It's just too wonderful for words'; 'It is beyond human telling'. All this is true. But it is not going to be of much help to your friend, who is wondering what *can* be said about the love of God.

Now see how the incarnation changes all this. No longer are you at a loss for words. You can ask your friend to imagine Jesus trudging his lonely and painful way to the cross, there to die in shame and agony – not for anything *he* did, but for our sake. Imagine the love which this action shows. <u>It is like someone laying down their life in order that another might live. This is what the love of *God* is like.</u> Can you see the new depth, clarity and quality which is given to your statements about the character of God in this way? You aren't talking about abstract ideas any more – you are talking about poignant and powerful events in a real life, which have the power to move and change lives even today.

<u>The second thing which God achieved through the cross is that *he brings home to us how much he loves us*.</u> In order to appreciate this point, think about the nature of God himself. It is very easy to picture God as the high king of heaven, exalted above the rough and tumble of this everyday world. He might be distant and remote, aloof from the worries and problems of this world. He might be too exalted to be concerned about his creation. The doctrine of the incarnation speaks movingly of the *humility* of God. The creator

of the world chose to enter into his world, not as a Roman emperor at the seat of imperial power, but as a child born in squalor somewhere in the backwaters of the empire. God humbled himself, stooping down to meet us where we are – and we must humble ourselves, if we are to meet him.

Above all, the place at which we see God humbling himself is on the cross itself. Once we have realised that it is none other than the Son of God who is dying on the cross, a whole new world opens up to us. People thought that God had abandoned Christ – but, in reality, he was there, working out the salvation of the world. The crowds around the cross called on Jesus to save himself – but he stayed there to the bitter end, and saved us instead. He bore his suffering on account of his love for us. The Son of God willingly died for people like you and me. Now we might be able to understand someone giving his life for especially good people. But the amazing thing is this: while we were still sinners, Christ died for us (Romans 5:8). As Paul puts it, 'I live by faith in the Son of God, who loved me and gave himself for me' (Galatians 2:20).

Suppose you care for someone very much, but they don't seem to appreciate this. Try to imagine what you could do to impress on them how much you love them. You could tell them about your feelings towards them. That might help. But we all know that actions speak louder than words! A more impressive way of showing love would be to *do* something – like giving them something special. And, in the end, the greatest thing that anyone can give for anyone else is their own life (John 15:13). And that is what we see happening in the cross. God gives us the most precious thing he possesses – his own Son – to show us how much he loves us (John 3:16). 'This is love ... that [God] loved us and sent his Son as an atoning sacrifice for our sins' (1 John 4:10).

But there is more to the cross than this. God loves us
– and part of that love is his firm purpose and power to
change us, to get us out of the mess we are in on account
of sin. That means dealing with the *penalty*, the *power*,
and the *presence* of sin. A third vital aspect of what God
was doing on the cross, then, can be summed up like
this. God *was breaking the stranglehold of sin in our
lives*. The obedient life, suffering and death of the Son of
God delivers us from the penalty of sin, begins to break
the power of sin, and will one day finally deliver us from
the presence of sin. Through the cross of Christ, God
sets in motion a chain of events. Some of those events
have already happened; some are in the process of happening; some have yet to happen in all their fullness.

What was God doing on the cross? In the fourth
place, he was *liberating us from the fear of death*. So
much of Western culture is terrorised by the fear of
death. People find it difficult even to talk about death,
because it is so threatening a subject. Yet through his
cross and resurrection, Jesus liberates his people from
this dreadful fear. Jesus shares our human nature, so
that 'by his death he might destroy him who holds the
power of death – that is, the devil – and free those
who all their lives were held in slavery by their fear of
death' (Hebrews 2:14–15). Through Christ's death and
resurrection, God has gained a great and famous victory over death. And that victory can be ours! Listen to
Paul, as he concludes the great exposition of the reality
and relevance of his resurrection in 1 Corinthians 15:
'Thanks be to God! He gives us the victory through our
Lord Jesus Christ.' (verse 57).

Now there is much more that can be said about
the cross than this. A textbook would be required to
do justice to the many central themes of the gospel
which converge on the cross of Christ. The theme of
the reality of forgiveness would be of major importance, as would that of the costliness of forgiveness.

So too would the theme of the need for people to respond to the cross, to allow it to have an impact upon our fallen and broken lives.

The opening words of Charles Wesley's great hymn of praise, 'And can it be?', are worth thinking about here. The hymn opens with a question which I used to wonder about a lot myself.

> And can it be? That I should gain
> An interest in the Saviour's blood?

How can the death of Christ affect *me*? Now notice carefully Wesley's choice of words. He doesn't speak of 'my Saviour's blood', but about 'the Saviour's blood'. Why? Because he isn't your Saviour until you let him become your Saviour. He is someone else's Saviour. Martin Luther, the German reformer, made the same point, as he commented on those well-known words from Luke 2:11: 'Today in the town of David a Saviour has been born to you; he is Christ the Lord.' Luther emphasised that Christ is someone else's Saviour and someone else's Lord – unless *you* decide to let him become your Saviour and your Lord. Faith is about a decision to accept Christ, and all his benefits, and make them your own. It is a decision to feed upon the bread of life (John 6:48), and to drink deep of the spring of living water (John 4:14). It is a free and willing surrender to Christ, by which we allow ourselves to share in his sufferings, in order that we may finally share in his risen glory (Romans 8:17).

The same point is made very clearly by Paul's dramatic declaration that God 'gives us the victory through our Lord Jesus Christ' (1 Corinthians 15:57). He offers us something; we have to accept it and receive it. Faith is about accepting what God offers us through the cross of Christ. Imagine that you are offering a friend a precious gift. You stand there, patiently, your arms outstretched, as you hold this gift in front of him. 'Take it! It's yours!' But your friend makes no response. He won't accept your gift. Eventually, you turn away, saddened. To offer someone something precious doesn't mean that they will accept it. And through the cross, God is offering us something incredibly precious – so precious that his only Son died so that we could have it. We are offered forgiveness of our sins, victory over death, and a new life. But we must accept and receive this gift.

Looking back on my own life as a Christian, I can see that a turning point came when I realised that the cross of Christ wouldn't change me unless I allowed it to. I used to think that Christianity was about believing that certain things were true; for example, that the crucifixion really happened. I didn't realise that it could affect me personally. I didn't understand that this event in history could turn my own history inside out, and make it 'his story' for me.

Since then, I've noticed that many people have the same difficulty. They think of the cross as something which happened long, long ago and far, far away (all the best stories seem to begin like that!). If you're in that situation, maybe my own experience could be helpful. I found it very valuable to close my eyes, and imagine that I was there, standing amidst the crowd near Calvary, and watching Christ die. I would imagine that I was asking myself: why did this wonderful man have to die? And gradually, the rest of the crowd would fade away. I was the only one left. And a voice would say to me: '*You* are the reason why Christ had to die.'

So what was God doing on the cross? Many things, as we have seen. But this book is about suffering, and we must therefore ask how the cross relates to this theme. The most important answer of all for our purposes relates to the presence and participation of our God in suffering. God was present at Calvary.

He came down from the Balcony to the Road, and walked among us, suffering and wondering, like us. He knows what it is like to suffer at first hand. Faith provides us with this vital insight. Theology insists that we value and relish it.

So the creator enters into his creation – not as a curious tourist, but as a committed saviour. He does not observe it from the Balcony, but comes down to the level of the Road, to be with us. This astonishing act of self-emptying and humility is celebrated at the Christian festival of Christmas, when we recall that the one who, though rich beyond all splendour, became poor for our sake. As the Nicene Creed puts it, 'for us, and for our salvation, he came down from heaven'. We might think of some more lines from Charles Wesley's hymn, 'And Can It Be?'

> He left his father's throne above,
> So free, so infinite his grace.
> Emptied himself of all but love,
> And bled for Adam's helpless race.

The love of God expresses itself in the suffering of Christ, which leads to our redemption.

Now some will point out, rightly, that God knows everything. He does not need to experience suffering to know what it is like. But we can turn that observation on its head. For it reminds us, first, that God did not *need* to suffer to know what it was like. He *chose* to suffer. Why? Part of the answer lies in the fact that God 'accommodates himself to our weakness' (John Calvin). He knows that we find it difficult to accept that he, too, knows about suffering. So, for our benefit, he makes it as clear as we could hope that he knows. The crucifixion of Christ is a public demonstration that God knows suffering at first hand. It is there, in part, to reassure us of this point. God knows how weak our faith is, and does all he can to sustain and support it from his side.

Second, there is a real difference between knowing about something, and knowing it at first hand. I can know about suffering, by watching my friends who are in pain. But I am an observer, not a participant. I am on the Balcony, rather than the Road. Or I can know suffering at first hand, by experiencing it myself. As a young man, I remember people telling me how dreadfully painful migraine headaches were. Yet although I knew that these headaches were painful, this was a second-hand insight. I had yet to experience that pain myself. After my first experience of this kind of headache, I felt a new sympathy for those people. I knew at first hand what they had been through – and it hurt! We could call the first kind of knowledge 'cognitive', and the second 'experiential'.

I once got into conversation with a student who was in a state of depression. He found his situation difficult to cope with, for it seemed that there was little that could be done about it. At his bedside, he had a self-help book on 'how to live with depression'. It was written by someone who had himself been through a period of depression, and had subsequently put his experiences on paper. Every now and then, this student would read some passages from that book. He would feel much better for having done so. 'That's just how I feel! That person really understands me!' Such thoughts helped him cope with his depression, because he felt that someone else had made it through what he was currently experiencing. There was light at the end of the tunnel.

The passion stories of the gospels are like that self-help book. They bring the insights of the Balcony to those of us on the Road. They tell of someone who really understands suffering, and who has been through it himself. 'I can relate to that! Jesus Christ must know how I feel when I suffer. This is a real figure of flesh and blood who went through the same sorts of things that I experience! And if Jesus Christ really is God, then God must have experienced all this pain and misery at first hand himself. I can relate to this God.' Such thoughts bring us to one of the most moving features of the gospel. The God whom we know through Jesus Christ is compassionate and sympathetic. He *understands* us.

No discussion of suffering and the purposes of God can ignore the fact that God suffered in Jesus Christ. That vital theme will resonate throughout the rest of this book.

8

THE PRICE OF LIFE

An Oxford colleague and I had not met up for some time. We eventually arranged to get together for lunch one day, to have a chat. We talked about life, swapped news, and discussed our mutual friends – the sort of things any friends do when they get together after a period of absence. My friend then told me a story about a young woman who had been seriously injured in a traffic accident. Although she survived the accident, she would have to endure a degree of pain for the remainder of her life.

My friend was in a reflective mood. I remember him saying something like, 'She was so badly hurt, she is probably going to be in some pain for the rest of her days. You know, if she had been an animal – a horse or a dog – she would have been put to sleep.' That remark stayed in my mind, even though (I have to confess) I have forgotten just about everything else we talked about that day.

Suffering is the price we pay for being alive. More than that; it is the price we pay for being human. We are willing to terminate the life of an animal to prevent it suffering. But human life is different. Human existence seems to be something priceless. Suffering does not make life meaningless or valueless. Suffering is part of life – not an add-on feature which we can dispense with, but a vital aspect of our existence as humans. To eliminate suffering is to eliminate life itself. It would be to live in a pretend world, under permanent sedation from its trials and tribulations – but also from its joys and pleasures.

But there is more to it than this. Suffering brings us to maturity. We learn through suffering. There is much truth in the old Greek saying '*pathemata mathemata* – suffering is education'. <u>Suffering makes us more sensitive and compassionate people, more aware of the needs and anxieties of others. It brings out the full power of human creativity</u>. It is no accident that most of the best novels seem to arise from situations of pain or hardship. Van Gogh's paintings echo his personal sadness. Some of Beethoven's greatest music dates from the period of his life when he was devastated by the thought of becoming deaf, and thus being cut off from the musical world of his own making.

Suffering often brings out the full potential of human beings, unleashing a creativity which is too easily stifled by smugness and security. Orson Welles is merely one of many writers to note that material well-being and affluence seem to suppress the power of the human imagination. Renaissance Italy, with all its struggles and suffering, produced some of the finest works of art humanity has ever known. But what, Welles asked, had pampered, neutral and prosperous Switzerland ever contributed to the history of human culture? The cuckoo clock.

To be human is to want to be free. Freedom matters to people. Think of how many wars have been fought in order to preserve, or restore, the freedom of nations. Think of the great civil rights protests, which demanded freedom for the citizens of these nations. The yearning for liberty seems to be a basic feature, not merely of human civilization, but of human nature itself.

I remember once hearing an interview with a prominent politician in a small eastern European nation, demanding freedom from its much larger neighbour, then known as the Soviet Union. The interviewer pressed him on a significant point. What about the economic consequences of this? Wouldn't it spell economic ruin to break away from its larger neighbour? 'Maybe – but we want to be free to make our own mistakes!' was the indignant reply.

There is much in that reply. Children leave their parental home, setting to one side its familiarity and security. Why? Partly because they want to break free from it. However much they may value their parents, they want to live their own lives, to make their own decisions, and to learn from their own mistakes. Deep down, all of us know of our need to learn things for ourselves. We don't want to accept everything on authority. That seems too much like a lapse into blind and mindless dictatorship. We want to check things out for ourselves. And that means having the freedom to do so.

But what is the price of this freedom? Freedom implies that we are free to make mistakes; to do things which hurt others; to cause evil. Jean-Paul Sartre, easily among the most perceptive of the existentialist writers, spoke of humans as being 'condemned to freedom'. In other words, we have no choice but to be free, and to live with the consequences of that freedom. If we were simply a form of machine or computer, programmed to do only things that we found acceptable, there would be no problem about evil. We wouldn't do wrong things. We wouldn't be *allowed* to do them. We wouldn't cause suffering or evil. But then we wouldn't be free, either.

So we have two options: to be free in a restricted sense of the word (only to do good), or to be free in a fuller sense of the word (including the worrying possibility of being free to make mistakes, and do evil). The first is fraught with the risk of paternalism. 'Don't do this. It wouldn't be good for you.' The original sin of Genesis chapter 3 is based on a rejection of precisely this sort of freedom. The first man and woman were free to do exactly what they pleased – providing they did not do something which they were told was off limits.

But they did it. They didn't want to be told what was off limits, and what wasn't. They wanted to be like God – free to decide what was right and what was wrong. They wanted to set their own limits, and live within them. The Christian tradition has seen in this act of disobedience the root of all suffering: the demand that we be free to choose for ourselves, and act accordingly. It seems that a central element of fallen human nature is a rugged sense of independence: we do not like being told what we may and may not do.

So we have freedom – a freedom to do evil, a freedom to avoid and disobey God. God leaves us room to be human. He makes space for us to make mistakes. God pulls himself back from his creation, in order to allow it to exercise the freedom which he chose to allow it. It is pointless to speak of God endowing his creatures with freedom, only to refuse to allow them to exercise that freedom. And in the exercise of that freedom, we may see the origins of much of the tragic suffering of the world.

It is no accident that the two nations which probably inflicted more suffering upon humanity than any others – Nazi Germany and the Stalinist Soviet Union – both deliberately and persistently ignored God, dismissing him as something of an irrelevant sentimental fool whose ideas were out of place in the brave new world of the 1930s and 1940s. Looking back on those grim days, that observation now seems more of a criticism of the 1930s and 1940s, rather than of God.

But would we rather be without that freedom? Paradoxically, it is something that we can never abandon,

even though we find it difficult to live with its results. As Sartre rightly saw, to be human is to be
free to commit evil and to inflict suffering. Part of
our problem with suffering is that we are reluctant
to allow that there is something wrong with human
nature. We find it difficult to accept that there could
be a flaw in human nature, which allows us to abuse
our God-given freedom to godless and inhuman ends.
Yet the casualty of this observation is not God; it is
humans who persist in their deluded and naive belief
about the goodness of human nature.

There is another aspect of suffering which we need
to note here. This is the sheer tragedy of the human
predicament. That word tragedy needs explanation. In
everyday use, it tends to mean something like disastrous, pitiful or pathetic. But here it means more
than that. It points to our powerlessness to change
things. It hints at our lack of control over our own
destiny. It declares our inability to change things, and
our sense of anger, mingled with despair, at the way
things are. Part of the offence of suffering lies in the
fact that we cannot control it. Suffering is part of the
chaos, the disorder, of sin. We may have been able
to master the skills of putting people on the moon,
and discovering the hidden secrets of the most distant planets. But, back home, we cannot put an end
to human suffering. One of the reasons why modern
human beings find suffering so offensive is that its
existence points to the limits of human achievement.
Suffering remains unmastered and untamed – despite
all human advances in civilization.

Many cultures have developed ways of coping with
the tragic side of life. They know that nature is difficult to control and predict. Suffering takes its place
among the changes and chances of life. Suffering does
not seem to have been a major philosophical problem in the Middle Ages, nor is it today for countless

millions in Africa and Latin America. But in the highly
developed societies of the West, suffering is a problem, perhaps because these societies have long lost
sight of cultural resources for coping with suffering.
It is not so much a theological, as a cultural, issue. So
how has this problem arisen?

In the West, and especially in the United States,
a form of 'cultural Pelagianism' has gained the up-
per hand. Pelagianism was a movement, based at
Rome in the early fifth century, which asserted that
human beings were in total control of their situation,
including their relationship to God. To its critics, this
overconfident worldview overlooked the tragic side
of human nature, with its obvious weaknesses and
failings. Pelagianism was, at heart, a delusion – but
a delusion which many people passionately wanted to
believe in. They didn't want to face up to the hard facts
of life, which suggested that human beings were not in
control of things, and needed the grace of God if they
were to survive and prosper.

Just as Pelagius declared that human beings had
total control over themselves and their destinies, so
modern Western society wants to believe that it can
control every aspect of its being. Yet although it is
enormously technologically advanced, Western society
has discovered that it cannot defeat death any more
than it can control suffering. Here, again, we have a
deeply attractive delusion. Many people want to believe in the perfectibility of society, and the essen-
tial goodness of human nature. And they close their
eyes to the harsh facts of life, of which suffering is
one, which suggest they are living in a make-believe
world.

Suffering thus causes offence, by pricking this bubble
of optimism. It is a painful reminder of the limitations of human nature and human culture. Suffering
hurts, because it points to definite and disconcerting

limits to human abilities. At least some of the theological fuss about suffering reflects this sense of outrage and offence. It is this which explains the paradox that Westerners – those who are among the most privileged of the human race, who enjoy standards of living which are astonishing by other standards, and who, through excellent medical services, suffer less than anyone else – make suffering into a bigger theological problem than it need be.

So how should Christians respond to this? Partly, by asking that we recover our awareness of our limitations as human beings. Suffering is something threatening because it is a reminder of our powerlessness to control our world. We need to accept those limitations, and realise that, on account of them, suffering will be an inevitable part of human existence. It is the price we pay for being human. And that leads us to consider the place of suffering in the life of the one who, in the eyes of Christians, is the only perfect human being ever to have lived.

A naive view of suffering would expect that Christ, as the perfect human being, would know no pain or suffering. But the truth is far more impressive than this Utopian delusion. Socrates may have shown us how to suffer with dignity; Christ shows us how to suffer with hope.

9

SUFFERING AND JESUS CHRIST

At the heart of any Christian understanding of suffering is not a collection of abstract thoughts about God, but a committed, active reflection upon Jesus Christ. The cross holds the key to the Christian understanding of suffering. To develop this point a little, we may ask: What is the love of God like? Some theology textbooks give answers along the following lines: the love of God is infinite, invisible, and intangible. It is beyond the scope of human language to describe. Now that is true, but it is not especially helpful. If God is indeed love, we want to be able to savour that love for ourselves, and tell others of what that love is like. We need to be able to picture it in some way. To know what the love of God is like is not merely to learn more about God – it is to discover more about love itself.

The knowledge that God became incarnate in Christ is good news for all of us who want to say what God is like, rather than ramble on about what he is *not* like. A cluster of scintillating biblical images bring out this point superbly. Christ is 'the image of the invisible God' (Colossians 1:15). Nobody has ever seen God – but Christ makes him known, in a visible and tangible form (John 1:18). Here is God in the flesh, God making himself known in a personal form. The one who fashioned the creation enters into that same creation, now sold into sin, in order to buy it back.

Again, Christ 'is the radiance of God's glory and the

exact representation of his being' (Hebrews 1:3). In other words, Christ represents exactly what God is like, as a medal or coin might bear the exact likeness of a king, president or ruler. In Palestine, coins bore the image of the Roman emperor of the day – an emperor who was far off and distant, unknown to virtually all the native population (Matthew 22:19–20 draws on this point). In much the same way, Christ makes a seemingly far-off and distant God draw close, by disclosing what he is like to us.

Charles Wesley spoke of Christ being 'our God contracted to a span' – in other words, a scaled-down medal of God. John Calvin spoke of God accommodating himself to our abilities, and thus making himself known in forms that we can grasp and understand. In Christ, God comes down to our level, meeting us where we are. Christ is like a statue (Origen), allowing us to hold an image of God before our eyes, and meditate upon it. For Paul, this thought brings home still further the immensity of the love of God for sinners. Even while we were still sinners – before we repented, or improved ourselves – Christ died for us. God may indeed hate sin; he nevertheless loves sinners.

In human terms, the greatest demonstration of love human beings can manage is usually their last, as well as their greatest – they give the greatest thing which they possess – the precious gift of life itself. 'Greater love has no-one than this, that he lay down his life for his friends' (John 15:13). I remember vividly the first time I heard the pathetic story of a medical orderly caught up in the brutality of the First World War. He was crouching in the security of his trench somewhere in Flanders, when he saw one of his comrades fall wounded some distance from the safety of his own lines. Rather than leave him to die, the medical orderly crawled the considerable distance to where the man lay, and, with great difficulty, dragged him back.

As the orderly lowered his friend into the trench, he himself was hit by a sniper's bullet, and mortally wounded. As he lay dying, he was told that his friend would live, and he was able to die with that knowledge. He had given his life for a friend. Doubtless many other examples of this sort of behaviour in battle could be given. It illustrates human love forced to its absolute limits, in that the man who gives his life for his friend does not even enjoy the satisfaction of his future company. All is given, and nothing received – except, perhaps, an all too brief satisfaction that something worth while has been achieved.

In the death of Jesus Christ on the cross, we can see the amazing love of God revealed to a wondering world. Christ is God in human flesh; in the image of the dying Christ, we see God himself, giving himself up for his people. Charles Wesley exults in this thought:

> Amazing love! how can it be
> That thou, my God, shouldst die for me?

and

> 'Tis mystery all! th'immortal dies!
> Who can explore his strange design?
> In vain the first-born seraph tries
> To sound the depths of love divine!

Here is no surrogate, no representative, no delegation. Here is God himself, willingly giving himself for us, in order that we might have life in all its fullness.

One of the most powerful pieces of reflection upon the meaning of the cross was written before AD 750 in Old English, and is widely known as the 'Dream of the Rood' ('rood' is the Old English, or Anglo-Saxon, word for 'cross'). In this poem, the writer tells of how he dreamed 'the best of dreams', in which he saw a cross studded with the jewels and richness of victory:

> It was as though I saw a wondrous tree
> Towering in the sky, diffused with light.

Yet as he wonders at this 'glorious tree of victory', it changes its appearance before his eyes, appearing to become covered with blood and gore. How can it be that this strange tree should have two so very different appearances? And as he wonders, the cross begins to speak for itself, telling him its story. It tells of how it was once a young tree, growing in a forest, only to be chopped down, and taken to a hill. When it had been firmly put in its place, a hero came, and voluntarily climbed him:

> Then the young hero (who was God almighty)
> Got ready, resolute, and strong in heart.
> He climbed onto the lofty gallows-tree,
> Bold in the sight of all who watched,
> For he intended to redeem us all.

Before his eyes, the young hero is pierced with dark and cruel nails. The tree is pierced by these same nails, and drenched with the blood which pours from the gaping holes they tear in his flesh. Yet through this appalling suffering victory is gained, and humans are set free.

> . . . May God be friend to me
> He who suffered once upon the gallows-tree
> Here on earth for our sins. He redeemed us
> And granted us our life and heavenly home.

Too often, we limit our thinking about the cross to its effects on us. But what about its effect on God? Try to imagine, however dimly, the effect that the death of his only Son must have had upon God. The Son suffers physical pain, a sense of separation from the Father, and a cruel and lingering death. The Father suffers the agony of seeing his Son taken captive and crucified by his own creation. We must not hesitate to speak of the pain of God at the death of his Son. That death and that pain are for real. Yet God is prepared to suffer that pain and grief, on account of what it brings in its wake – our redemption. 'For God so loved the world that he gave his one and only Son, that whoever believes in him shall not perish but have eternal life' (John 3:16). The Spirit, the bond of love between Father and Son, is caught up in the suffering of both, and the entire Godhead – Father, Son and Spirit – are brought together in the pain of the loving redemption of sinful humanity. The cost of that redemption is enormous – but so is the love that underlies and motivates that glorious and gracious act of salvation. 'This is how God showed his love among us: He sent his one and only Son into the world that we might live through him . . . he loved us and sent his Son as an atoning sacrifice for our sins' (1 John 4:9–10).

Suffering causes problems for Christians to the extent that it seems to call into question the loving kindness of God. Might not God turn out to be some terrible divine sadist, who actually enjoys inflicting pain on his people? Or maybe he has not the slightest interest in us, not caring whether we suffer or not. But our reflections on the love of God for sinners put an end to both these options. <u>God is passionately committed to our wellbeing, and shares in our sufferings and pain in order to redeem us, and finally to deliver us from their presence.</u> In Christ, God experienced suffering in all its apparent meaninglessness – and yet brought good out of it, for Christ himself and for all who trust in him.

The love of God revealed in and through the death of the suffering Christ thus graciously soothes our anxieties, by declaring firmly that suffering has, by the grace of God, its place within his redemptive purposes. The early Church was passionately concerned to safeguard insights such as these. One particular threat was posed by the heresy known as docetism. This taught that Jesus was not really human at all. He just seemed to suffer. He just seemed to be in pain. (The word 'docetism' comes from the Greek verb *dokein*, meaning 'to seem'.) Rightly, the theologians of the early Church saw that it was vital to defend the reality of the suffering and death of Christ. If they were not for real, then he did not really confront the forces of evil which threaten us.

Here, then, is the love of God. It is a love which knows no limits in its determination to break down all the barriers to our having all that God wants for us. It shows the compassion of our God for us as fallen and sinful creatures – a theme which dominates the chapter which follows.

10

THE COMPASSION OF OUR GOD

We tend to read Scripture too quickly. Certainly, there are some passages which need to be gulped down, like a refreshing and cooling drink on a hot day. But there are others which need to be sipped and savoured slowly, as if they were a classic vintage. One such passage is that which opens one of Paul's most reflective letters, in which the themes of human suffering and divine consolation compete for attention:

> Praise be to the God and Father of our Lord Jesus Christ, the Father of compassion and the God of all comfort, who comforts us in all our troubles, so that we can comfort those in any trouble with the comfort we ourselves have received from God. For just as the sufferings of Christ flow over into our lives, so also through Christ our comfort overflows (2 Corinthians 1:3–5).

God is *compassionate*. The word comes from the Latin, has the basic meaning of 'suffering alongside someone', and thus possesses extended meanings such as 'kindness', 'consideration' or 'clemency'. To be compassionate is to be able to set yourself alongside one who is suffering, to share their pain and anguish. The word 'sympathetic' has much the same meaning, but derives from the Greek. Christ is our sympathetic high priest (Hebrews 4:15). He has been through all that we are being asked to go through. Knowing that, we may approach him with confidence. Why? Because he understands our plight. Indeed, he has shared it, and thus created a powerful bond of sympathy between himself and ourselves.

This thought provides us with more than spiritual insight and consolation. It also gives us a real stimulus to alleviate suffering. Why? What new reason does it provide for working to rid the world of its suffering? Because the suffering of the world affects God. It grieves him. The pages of history are stained with the tears of God. By working to relieve suffering in the world, we are lessening the sadness of God, who shares in that suffering. Our suffering is his suffering; his suffering is our suffering. Perhaps the face of the crucified Christ, shot through with pain and tears, allows us to envisage how God must feel over the way his creation is groaning in pain as it awaits its liberation from bondage to decay (Romans 8:20–2).

This thought gives us a powerful motive to work for the relief of pain and suffering in the world. Many Christians find the overt secularism of many relief agencies disconcerting, and for this reason are less committed to caring for the needs of others than they might otherwise be. But theology has an insight which must be heard here. By seeking to alleviate the hardships suffered by others in this harsh world, we are working to ease the pain of God at the suffering of his creation. God suffers along with his people. By lessening their sadness and suffering, we are bringing a smile to the face of God. It does not really matter whether this takes the form of caring for the needs of our neighbours who are old and infirm, or giving money to avert global famines and floods, or spending time talking with those who are sad and lonely. By doing any of these, we are meeting a real human need, we are fulfilling the command to love as we have been loved, and we are gladdening the father-heart of a God who chooses to suffer along with those whom he created and loves.

And in his love for us, God consoles us in our suffering. I often find my mind going back to one of the great prophetic passages of the Old Testament, which converges upon and is fulfilled by the death of Jesus Christ – the prophecy of the Suffering Servant of God (Isaiah 52:13–53:12). It is impossible to read this passage without being reminded of the last hours of the life of Christ. Suffering, shame and pain cast their shadow over the entire section.

The passage appears to open with the theme of exaltation: 'See, my servant will act wisely; he will be raised and lifted up and highly exalted' (52:13). This might immediately suggest that the servant of God will find fame, fortune and favour in life. But soon the darker side of the theme becomes clear. Christ is indeed exalted and lifted up – he is lifted up on the cross at Calvary, for all to see and despise, in the most public and painful form of execution. 'I, when I am lifted up from the earth, will draw all men to myself' (John 12:32), he predicts.

The themes of rejection, being reviled and undergoing suffering soon come to the fore. 'He was despised and rejected by men, a man of sorrows, and familiar with suffering' (53:3). The suffering servant shares our human situation, drinking deeply of the bitter waters of pain and affliction. The poignancy of the passage is unmistakable. It sketches, briefly and yet with great effect, the image of a tender young life destroyed through suffering. Perhaps the thought of the utter pointlessness of it all passes through our minds.

Almost anticipating such a development, the passage moves on to reflect on the purpose of this innocent suffering: 'Surely he took up our infirmities and carried our sorrows, yet we considered him stricken by God, smitten by him, and afflicted. But he was pierced for

our transgressions, he was crushed for our iniquities;
the punishment that brought us peace was upon him,
and by his wounds we are healed' (53:4–5). The first
statement is astonishing, and pulls us up short. The
servant is suffering, not on behalf of himself, but for
us. But how? And why? The servant has the sorrow
of a sinful world laid upon his shoulders, in much the
same way as the priest laid the sins of his people upon
the scapegoat, before driving it into the wilderness.

In some way, the servant has taken upon himself the
burden of our grief and sorrow. Those looking on rush to
the wrong conclusion. He has been condemned by God!
But subsequent events make it clear that this is not the
case. In some way, it is *we* who have been condemned,
and the suffering servant who bears our punishment.
Suffering has been taken away from us, and laid upon
him. Through the mystery of God's compassion and
care, the servant is prepared to suffer in order that
others might be thought of as being righteous (53:11).
He was content to be treated as if he were a sinner,
bearing their sin, and suffering beside them (53:12).

This passage, perhaps more powerfully than any
other, brings out the idea of the compassion of Christ.
He is prepared to suffer alongside sinners, being reck-
oned among their number. Remember that there were
three crosses at Calvary. When Christ was crucified,
they executed a convicted criminal on either side of him.
Of the evangelists, it is Luke who draws our attention
to the full significance of this point. Jesus was utterly
innocent of any crime; indeed, one of the two criminals,
astonished that Jesus was being executed with them,
turned to the other, and said: 'We are punished justly,
for we are getting what our deeds deserve. But this man
has done nothing wrong' (Luke 23:41). Furthermore,
the officer in charge of the execution squad, astonished
at the events unfolding before his eyes, declared 'Surely
this was a righteous man' (Luke 23:47).

Yet Jesus died between two criminals – men who were sinners in the eyes of the world: 'there they crucified him, along with the criminals – one on his right, the other on his left' (Luke 23:33). What more dramatic symbol could one want of the compassion of Christ, when he suffered alongside sinners? Or what more convincing fulfilment of Christ's declaration that 'It is written: "And he was numbered with the transgressors"; and I tell you that this must be fulfilled in me' (Luke 22:37). Christ was – *and was meant to be* – present with those who suffered and finally died.

This is compassion in the full sense of the word. Here we see Jesus being prepared to suffer with sinners, being counted as if he were among their number, and condemned to share their fate. And he accepted this identification. There was no attempt to evade its consequences. He identified with us right up to the end, joining us in this solidarity of suffering.

God has borne our sorrows on the bitter cross of Calvary. He became acquainted with our grief. This is no vague mumbling about God 'being aware' of our sufferings; it is a glorious affirmation that God has shared our sufferings, injecting the fragrance of his redeeming presence into the darker side of our existence. God is a fellow-sufferer who understands, not someone who views our situation from a safe distance, uncomprehendingly.

We need to distinguish between the related (but different) ideas of 'sympathy' and 'empathy'. Sympathy is the situation of having been through the same experience as someone else. You have, so to speak, suffered with them. In professional counselling, however, empathy is of paramount importance. In order to be of use to someone who needs comforting, you try to think yourself into their situation, and ask: 'How must they be feeling if they have been through this experience?' For example, suppose the person you are trying to help is dying from cancer. You, however, are perfectly fit. You try to work out what it must feel like to be dying of cancer, and thus to say and do things which might well be of some use to the unfortunate person on the receiving end of your well-intentioned ministrations.

But try to place yourself in the place of the person who is in real need. For example, suppose that your mother has recently died, and you find yourself distressed as a result. You want to talk to someone about it. Which would you expect to find the more approachable and helpful: someone whose mother is still alive, but who is prepared to think themselves into your situation, and imagine how you must feel? Or someone whose mother died not that long ago, and who instinctively knows just how you feel about it? It is basic to human nature to prefer to talk to someone who shares your suffering – who *sympathises*. And that simple observation has important theological consequences.

Christ does not empathise with our sufferings, trying to work out how we must feel about the sorrows and woes of human existence. He already knows. He has been through them himself. He has experienced them at first hand. In short: he *sympathises* with us. And that brings a new depth and quality to our prayer to Christ in such situations. We can pray to him with confidence, knowing that he already knows our needs, and has experienced them before us. Are we troubled by temptation? Christ has been through a more severe time of testing than anything we are ever likely to experience. Christ 'has been tempted in every way, just as we are – yet was without sin' (Hebrews 4:15). Are we troubled by suffering and pain? Remember that Christ suffered the agony of crucifixion. He knows what it is like.

There is a splendid story once told about shepherds in East Anglia, formerly the centre of England's wool trade. When a shepherd died (so the story goes) he

would be buried in a coffin stuffed full of wool. Now the
real reason for this was probably to provide a market for
wool in a time of economic depression during the Middle
Ages. But people found this rather practical explanation a little unexciting and unimaginative. Another
explanation was soon found for the practice, which
wove a little theology into what would otherwise have
been a thoroughly material matter.

The new explanation was this. When the day of
judgement came, Christ would notice the wool in the
coffin, and realise that this man had been a shepherd.
As he himself had once been a shepherd, he would know
the pressures the man had faced – the amount of time
needed to look after wayward sheep, and so on. So he
would understand why he hadn't been to church much!
The story makes an important point, which we must
treasure as one of the greatest of the gospel insights:
Christ knows our situation as one who is compassionate. Suffering is second nature to him. And we can thus
draw comfort and encouragement from him, as we face
the same in our own lives. The God of all compassion is
with us, even in the valley of the shadow of death.

But how can that shadow be lifted? Let us turn to
explore the theme of victory over suffering.

11

CHRIST'S VICTORY OVER SUFFERING

'Thanks be to God! He gives us the victory through our Lord Jesus Christ' (1 Corinthians 15:57). In what sense can the cross and resurrection of Christ be seen as a defeat of suffering? Exploring this question can open up ways of seeing the problem of suffering in a totally new light. The power of suffering lies partly in its presence, and partly in the terror that it instils. Suffering frightens us, for all sorts of reasons. It is a painful experience in its own right. Yet it also seems to imply other things – perhaps more frightening things.

An episode from my early childhood will illustrate my point. One morning, I woke up early to hear a strange noise in my bedroom. It sounded like someone knocking at my window. It was still dark. I was terrified. That sound – a mixture of knocking and scratching – made me bury myself deep under the bedclothes, in the hope that whoever it was would leave me alone, and go away. But the noise continued. Eventually morning came, and I plucked up enough courage to peek out of the bedclothes, and see what was going on.

It was a branch of a tree, snapped off by the wind during the night, which was scratching, scraping and tapping against the window. I felt a fool for being so frightened. Yet my reaction was understandable. I had heard a noise, which I could not explain. I had interpreted it in a way which I believed to be right – and which frightened me badly. When the morning came,

75

the noise remained – but I could see that it was not anything I should be worried about. My interpretation of the noise turned out to be incorrect. It was not the noise itself, but the fear of the unknown, the dreadful anxiety that the noise might be caused by something sinister, that had prompted me to dive under the bedclothes.

Suffering is like that. As a physical experience, it is vastly more painful and difficult to bear than a mere noise. But it is what suffering might *imply* that frightens many people. Suffering could imply meaninglessness. It could imply sin and separation from God, as Job's comforters knew only too well. It could imply that God is powerless to do anything about his world, or that he does not care for his creatures. These are some of the frightening implications of suffering. Suffering thus possesses a double cutting edge: the sheer pain and distress of the experience is driven to an unbearable intensity by what that suffering might imply.

Christ's death and resurrection draw the sting of suffering. They declare that suffering is not meaningless; God worked out the salvation of the world through the suffering of Christ. Suffering does not always result from sin, or lead to separation from God; the suffering of the sinless Christ, and his resurrection to glory, make this point more powerfully than we could ever have hoped for. Through faith, we are bonded to Christ, in a 'fellowship of sharing in his sufferings' (Philippians 3:10). And suffering does not mean that this world lies beyond the power or love of God. The almighty God stoops down in humility to suffer for us, to show us the full extent of his love for us.

And so, just as the dawn allowed me to stop worrying about the noise at my window, the dawn of the world's new day through the resurrection of Christ stills our anxieties about the sinister implications of suffering. It remains a painful and powerful presence in our world – but its sting has been drawn. It is seen in a new light. The element of the unknown, the sinister, has been removed. We are reassured that suffering does not possess the power we once thought. The bluff of suffering has been called. Its power, though not its presence, has been defeated.

Suffering is defeated, not in the sense of being abolished, but in the sense of being turned around. Suffering – along with its ally, death – tries to separate us from God, breaking our links with him, and severing our life-giving fellowship with him. But through the cross, suffering has been humiliated. The suffering of Christ proves to be the grounds of our union with God – a union of sympathy which nothing can destroy. Suffering was once seen as our enemy, something which separated us from God. It can now be seen as something which can bring us closer to God.

Furthermore, we can rejoice in the sure and certain hope, grounded in the resurrection of Christ and sealed by the Holy Spirit, that one day we shall be delivered from the *presence* of suffering. There is a 'not-yet' element to the victory of Christ over sin, death and suffering. That hope can keep us going (and keep us *growing*!) in times of hardship. An analogy might be helpful, as we explore this important point.

Human history and Christian experience tell us of a constant struggle against suffering and pain in our own lives, even as Christians. There is a real danger, it would seem, that talking about 'the victory of faith' will become nothing more than empty words, signifying nothing other than a contradiction between faith and experience. How can we handle this problem?

One of the most helpful ways of dealing with this difficulty is suggested by the Second World War. Although the memory of this period of history becomes increasingly distant with every year that passes, its atmosphere is powerfully evoked in countless motion pictures and novels. As a result, those who never lived through this period in history are able to experience its tensions and hopes, and gain an understanding of what was happening at this time.

The victory won over sin through the death of Christ was like the liberation of an occupied country (such as France or Norway) from Nazi rule towards the end of that war. In order to appreciate the full power of these analogies, we need to try to think ourselves into the mindset of an occupied European country during the Second World War. We need to allow our imaginations to take in the sinister and menacing idea of an occupying power. Life has to be lived under the shadow of this foreign presence. And part of the poignancy of the situation is its apparent utter hopelessness. People thought that nothing could be done about it.

Now imagine the electrifying news. There has been a far-off battle. Some call it D-Day. And it is turning the tide of the war. A new phase of the war is opening up, in which the occupying power is in disarray. Its back has been broken. In the course of time, the Nazis will be driven out of every corner of occupied Europe.

But the Nazis are still present in the occupied country. In one sense, the situation has not changed. But in another, more important, sense, the situation has changed totally. The scent of victory and liberation is in the air. A total change in the psychological climate results. I remember once meeting a man who had been held prisoner in the Japanese prisoner-of-war camp at Changi in Singapore. He told me of the astonishing change in the camp atmosphere which came about when one of the prisoners (who owned a short-wave radio) learned of the collapse of the Japanese war effort in the middle of 1945. Although all in the camp still remained prisoners, they knew that their enemy had been beaten. It was only a matter of time before they were released. And those prisoners, I was told, began to laugh and cry, as if they *were* free, even though freedom had yet to come their way.

We remain captives in a world of suffering, as those prisoners remained incarcerated in that compound at Changi. Yet the hope of liberation is at hand. The promise to be removed from its imprisonment has been heard, and has been made credible by the death and resurrection of Christ. We wait – but we wait in hope.

There is another aspect of Christ's victory over suffering. There is a day-to-day, moment-by-moment victory, which Christ died to make possible. Each time we suffer, we are being offered an opportunity to claim a small victory over suffering. How? By not allowing it to intimidate us. By not allowing it to succeed in breaking our trust in God. But more than that: we can allow God to speak to us through that suffering. We can allow him to transform us, and to show us new depths of relationships with him, and with others. How? Let us meditate on the ways in which God can use suffering.

12

SUFFERING AND SPIRITUAL GROWTH

What is the positive role of suffering in our lives? In a logical or philosophical sense, the *fact* of suffering is neutral. The important thing is what we make of it – both in terms of how we *understand* it, and how we allow it to *affect* us. Here is where theology helps; it allows us to see suffering in a positive light, as a means of growth rather than as something meaningless. Suffering *can* become something meaningless and pointless – if we let it. But that same suffering could also be handled in a very different way. We could entrust it to God, in the firm belief that he will be able to use it. We must learn to offer our sufferings and distress to God, assured that he can, and will, use them to bring us to new depths of faith and service.

We have already seen how God has the remarkable ability to work through suffering in ways which may not at first have been apparent. The cross of Christ must be our model here, reminding us of how God was able to take what, to foolish human nature, seemed to be a disastrous and pointless episode of anguish, and bring good from it. So are we just going to endure suffering, letting it wash over us? Are we going to pretend that this major experience is not going to change us in any way? Are we going to deny God the opportunity to speak to us through this experience? Or are we going to discern something potentially beneficial and helpful within it?

Someone who is determined not to see any meaning within suffering will not learn anything from the experience. But someone who believes that God may be able to use suffering, to speak in it and through it, will be open to seeing the hand of God at work in this affliction. For Christians, God works through failure as much as through success, through suffering as much as through joy.

In an earlier chapter, we saw how suffering stripped away the delusions of security and immortality which seem to prevail outside the Christian faith. It peels away the veneer of assurance which can act as so powerful a barrier to the gospel. As a pastor, I have noticed how suffering can often be a way into the Christian faith. Often, the funeral of a partner proves to be a turning point in someone's spiritual journey, when the pieces of a complex puzzle suddenly fall into place. But it is not just those outside the Christian faith who can find their understanding of life transformed by suffering. It ought to be, above all, believers who grow through the experience of suffering. So how can Christians learn to understand how suffering can be handed over to God, with positive results? How can we grow through affliction?

In what follows, I shall take a series of biblical images, each charged with enormous potential for understanding the positive role that suffering can play within the Christian life. Again, I must stress that it is up to the believer to allow suffering to take on these roles. Suffering can lead to a refining of our faith – if we are prepared to allow God to do this. But it does not have to. Be open to God. Allow him to use what is happening to you, and redirect it. Explore what God might be saying to you through your experience. Learn to think positively, creatively and prayerfully about what you are going through.

1　The refinement of faith

The Old Testament often speaks of affliction or suffering in terms of the refining of faith. The imagery is powerful: in its crude state, a precious metal, such as silver or gold, contains substantial amounts of impurities, in the form of dross. The refiner's task is to remove this dross and, by doing so, to purify the metal, making it still more valuable. This is done by subjecting the metal to intense heat – for example, by passing it through a bed of white-hot coals. Suffering is seen as being like a refiner's fire, which removes the impurities from faith (eg, Isaiah 1:25; 48:10).

This way of thinking about the role of suffering in the Christian life has much to commend it. For example, only precious metals, like gold, were worth refining. Think of how precious your faith must be, if it is being refined by suffering (1 Peter 1:6–7). And realize how much more precious it will be, once all the dross has been removed.

Suffering gets rid of the dross of all the worldly supports we foolishly invent for our faith. Without realising it, we often allow these supports to take the place of God. It takes us, and sets us on our own with God. It strips away our assurance, and brings us face to face with God. With all the props of our faith stripped away, we learn to trust in God, and lean upon him alone. Too often, our faith rests on unreliable foundations – foundations such as satisfying personal relationships, a secure job, a healthy bank account, and physical health. Too easily, these become God-substitutes. 'Where your heart is, there is also your God' (Luther). Suffering or adversity strips them away, and obliges us to discover God all over again. It brings us back to him, by removing everything which we put in his place.

Perhaps this is what suffering might teach you about your life of faith. It might be helping you to realise how dependent your faith and hope have become on things which are *not* God – such as your material possessions – and offer you the opportunity to correct the situation.

2 The discipline of faith

Earlier, we spent some time reflecting about the nature of the love of God. That love is not something shallow and indulgent, which merely satisfies our fallen desires and short-term goals. The love of God is transformative, aiming to help us ultimately to achieve our chief end, which is 'to glorify God and enjoy him for ever' (Shorter Westminster Catechism). If the love of God is concerned to change us, to make us better, it must have the means available to do this. And one such means is discipline. Discipline enables us to keep hold of what we already possess of God, and to gain still more. Precisely because we are children of God by grace, we have the privilege of being disciplined by him: 'the Lord disciplines those he loves' (Hebrews 12:6; Proverbs 3:11–12).

Jesus Christ was the Son of God who 'learned obedience from what he suffered' (Hebrews 5:8). And, as children of God, we share, by faith, in all that Christ gained and achieved. Just as he suffered, so shall we suffer; just as he was glorified, so shall we be glorified. And just as he learned obedience through suffering, so must we learn obedience in the same way. It is a privilege which comes with being a child of God.

Now discipline is a word that is too easily misunderstood. Too often, it conjures up images of unjustified punishment, of sadistic schoolmasters, and of the cruel and heartless atmosphere of Victorian boarding schools (so powerfully and shamefully described by Charles Dickens and others). But these are not the associations of the biblical term. We need to look closely at what the biblical perspectives are on this matter.

Seen in its proper biblical context, discipline is

nothing other than (and nothing less than) training for the race of faith. Just as Christ was made perfect through suffering (Hebrews 5:8–9), so we who are united to him through faith must expect to share in his sufferings. Union with Christ through faith involves embracing the totality of Christ, not just those aspects that are easy to cope with! Suffering is integral, not optional, to those whose lives are, through the working of the Holy Spirit, being conformed to Christ.

But why do we need to be trained? A number of reasons come to mind. First, the Christian life is often compared to a battle. It is a struggle against sin, temptation, weakness, despair, confusion and doubt. It helps in this struggle to know that God is on our side, that we have been well armed by the grace of God (Ephesians 6:10–17), and that we are enabled ultimately to share in the victory which is ours through Christ. But the struggle goes on. If we are not to be overwhelmed, we must learn to be disciplined. A ragged and ill-disciplined army stands little chance against a determined opponent.

God has already given us much to enable us to survive, indeed, even to prosper, in this combat. But we must ensure that the resources given to us are matched by a personal dedication and commitment on our part. Discipline is a developed ability to cope with difficult situations, which is acquired through training and exposure to the sort of difficulties that lie ahead. Suffering and affliction hone our defences and strengthen our resolve to fight on against all the forces ranged against us which attempt to drag us back into the dusk of unbelief and lostness.

3 The pruning of a plant

One of the most powerful images of the manner in which Christians relate to Christ is that of the vine

(John 15:1–11). Christians are like branches on a vine. The image has many aspects. For example, we learn that unless a branch remains firmly attached to the stem of the vine, it will wither and die, and cease to bear fruit (15:4–6). The life-giving sap must be able to get through to the branch, if it is to grow and be fruitful. And so Christians must 'abide in Christ', remaining close to him and nestling in his presence, if they are to grow in grace and bear fruit in their lives. If a branch becomes detached from the vine, it will shrivel and wilt, and become like any other piece of dead wood, fit only for throwing away. Christians who wander from the nourishing and sustaining presence of Christ will end up withering in their faith, and losing their distinctiveness.

Now the vine grower is aware of how useless such branches are. If a branch does not bear any fruit, he will remove it. It has no useful purpose to play. But what is really interesting is what happens to branches that bear fruit. Does the vine grower leave them alone? No. In order to encourage and enable them to bear more fruit, he prunes them (15:2). Pruning is a tribute to the potential of a branch. It is an acknowledgement that it is already fruitful, and a recognition of its even greater capacity to bear fruit in the future. Pruning is not just a mark of favour; it is a mark of expectation and anticipation on the part of the vine owner.

Suffering is pruning. It is cutting off spurious growths, which might be of no value, or stopping shoots which, were they to grow further, would weaken the vine. It hurts the branch to be pruned. When you prune a rose, a fruit tree or a vine, you can see the wounds that you are inflicting upon it. But your pruning is not arbitrary, pointless and vindictive infliction of suffering upon an innocent and unsuspecting plant! It is an action designed to inflict the minimum of damage upon the plant, while at the same time achieving maximum enhancement of its potential.

Those who suffer may well be those who bear the most effective witness, and thus those who bear the most fruit in and through their Christian lives. If your suffering is pruning, see it as a mark of divine favour. Perhaps you are being prepared for growth and the bearing of much fruit.

4 The humility of faith

Humility is a central Christian virtue. The word comes from the Latin word *humus*, meaning 'earth'. To be humbled is to be brought down to earth, to be reminded of our lowly origins. It is also a much misunderstood word. For example, some Christians have the strange idea that humility means pretending that you have no God-given gifts or talents at all! And so, by sustaining this pretence, you end up declaring that God has given you no gifts of any kind. As a result, you become blind to the gifts that God has given you – gifts that are meant to be used in the building up of his Church.

Humility is a recognition that all we have, and all that we are, is a gift from God. Our gifts, talents and achievements are not something that we own or possess. They are not even things which we accomplish unaided. Rather, they are gracious gifts from God. They are an expression of the generosity of God, not of our deserving or merits. Humility does not deny that we have gifts or talents, but is an unpretentious willingness to admit that everything we have and everything that we are is the result of the grace of God, not only our efforts or achievements.

By recognising that all our resources for the Christian life come from God, we are enabled to avoid two of the worst pitfalls that occur in the Christian life. First, there is a failure to recognise that we rely totally upon

God for our spiritual survival and welfare. We begin to succumb to the attractive illusion that we can cope by ourselves. And by doing so, we cut ourselves off from the lifeline offered by God. If we think that we can look after ourselves, we don't bother looking anywhere else for support. Second, we become spiritually proud. We begin to think of things in terms of *our* achievements, *our* gifts, *our* talents, and so on. We lose sight of the fact that they are God's gifts, and that we are their stewards, not their owners. Our task is to make the best possible use of them, before returning them to their owner (the parable of the talents in Matthew 25:14–30 makes this point superbly).

Suffering humbles us. It reminds us that we do not have full control over our own situation. This is especially well illustrated in the life of the Swiss reformer Ulrich Zwingli. Zwingli was a pastor at Zurich in the year 1519, when the city was struck by an outbreak of the plague. Zwingli visited the sick regularly, and soon contracted the disease himself. As he lay on his sickbed, he realised that whether he lived or died lay totally beyond his control. He could not achieve his own recovery. He was powerless. 'Make what you will of me!' was his prayer. In the end, he recovered. But Zwingli's spirituality henceforth resonates with the theme of humility. It is God who achieves things for us, and who always offers to achieve more. Through his suffering, with all its attendant anxiety and uncertainty, Zwingli learned to look towards God for his security.

Suffering often brings home to us how powerless and helpless we are in the face of illness and death. A colleague of mine had become very old and ill, and was close to death. I went round to see him. He was quite happy to talk about his illness, and what its eventual outcome would be. I was enormously impressed by his courage, and found myself wondering if I would be able to match it when my turn came. But what I remember

most clearly from that discussion was the effect that
his debilitating illness had upon his understanding of
grace.

'I can't do anything for myself now. I have to rely
totally on the kindness of others.' He paused. 'The grace
of God has come to mean far more to me now than it ever
did before. It's like someone kind helping a helpless old
man like me.' In his utter helplessness, the idea of grace
had assumed a new reality and meaning. The idea had
come to life for him. 'Grace' wasn't just a word any more.
It was something on which his existence depended.
His reflections on his own predicament, brought about
by his illness, brought new depth to one of the most
familiar words of the gospel vocabulary.

5 Suffering provides opportunities for witness

The darkness of human suffering provides a window
through which the light of the Christian hope may
shine. Faith is something which affects our entire outlook on life, including the way in which we cope with
pain and affliction. Now suffering is often a public
event. Other people often notice the way in which we
react to hardship, illness, suffering and dying.

I used to work as a pastor in Nottingham, in England's
east Midlands. Part of my job was to officiate at funerals – as a result of which, I got to know most of the
staff at the city's various funeral homes. They often
talked about their work. One of the things that they
found most difficult was the first visit to the home of
the surviving relatives of the person who had died.
Sometimes it was a harrowing experience; at others,
it was not. 'You can usually tell fairly quickly whether
they are religious or not,' one commented (to general
assent). 'They seem so calm and peaceful, where anyone
else would have been having hysterics.'

Some of Paul's finest writing has its origin in some

form of captivity at Rome – possibly in prison, probably in some form of protective custody. On account of his having preached the gospel faithfully, Paul was 'suffering even to the point of being chained like a criminal' (2 Timothy 2:9). While taking comfort that the gospel itself could not be bound and imprisoned in this way, it is clear that Paul was distressed by the experience.

Distressed he may have been; but his affliction gave him new opportunities to witness to those round about him. 'What has happened to me has really served to advance the gospel' (Philippians 1:12). Everyone knew that he had been imprisoned on account of his faith in Christ, which thus provided him with a series of new opportunities to proclaim Christ. The point to be made is simple: in whatever situation we find ourselves, we are able to witness to the love of God in Christ. Suffering does not prevent us from affirming our faith and trust in God; indeed, it may open up new ways of doing so. The Christian Church has always recognised that dying, as well as living, provides believers with opportunities to declare their faith to the world. The North African Christian theologian Tertullian, writing in the early third century, remarked that 'the blood of the martyrs is the seed of the church'.

We have considered five possible ways in which suffering can be understood within the context of the Christian life. Suffering is part of the Christian life – a valuable and potentially productive aspect of that life, which leads to Christian maturity and the full stature of discipleship. But it must be seen in the right light before its maturing potential can be realised.

13

SHARING IN THE SUFFERING OF CHRIST

To be a Christian is to suffer *with* Christ and *for* Christ. Paul speaks powerfully of this aspect of faith in Christ:

> I consider everything a loss compared to the surpassing greatness of knowing Christ Jesus my Lord, for whose sake I have lost all things ... I want to know Christ and the power of his resurrection and the fellowship of sharing in his sufferings, becoming like him in his death (Philippians 3:8–10).

Read his words and *savour* them, turning them over in your mind as they cast light on the place of suffering in the Christian life. We could sum up much of what Paul is describing here by saying that the Christian life is *Christomorphic*. This, like many other words in the theologian's vocabulary, is a clumsy term. Yet its outward ugliness conceals an inner sweetness. For it expresses the idea that faith 'shapes us in the form of Christ'. Through faith, God breaks us and remoulds us, casting us in the shape of his own Son. The pattern of the life of Christ begins to make itself evident in our own lives, as we begin to live in ways that express his compassion and care, in the quiet confidence that we shall one day share also in his risen glory.

But there is a darker side to this. We who are being made like Christ must expect to share in his sufferings, before we share in his glory. Suffering and pain may

seem utterly pointless and meaningless – but then
Christ's death on the cross seemed much the same.
One of the most wonderful insights of the gospel is that
God is able to transfigure suffering which seems to have
no meaning and no purpose, and achieve something
through it. We may not know what is being achieved –
after all, those watching Christ die had no inkling of the
amazing events which were to follow in its wake. It may
seem to us, too, that our pain and hurt serve no purpose.
But that feeling unites us to Christ, in his pain and
sorrow at Calvary. The same God who brought purpose
and power out of the seemingly meaningless sufferings
of his Son is present, through faith, in our sufferings
today. We must learn to offer them to him, and ask him
to reassure us of his presence, power and purpose in
our own little scenes of crucifixion. So important is this
theme of suffering with Christ that we may consider it
in more detail in what follows.

The New Testament is shot through with the theme
of suffering – the sufferings of Christ on the cross, and
the sufferings of his people as they bear witness to him.
To be a Christian is to suffer. Christianity thus openly
acknowledges the reality and the pain of suffering.
It is something shared by the Father, the Son and
the children of God. Not for one moment is there a
suggestion that someone, by becoming a Christian,
can evade or escape from the world of suffering. No.
Christians may not be of the world; they nevertheless
remain in the world. There is no way in which coming
to faith involves being isolated from the suffering of the
world. Being redeemed from the world does not mean
being removed from the world.

Christians are in the world because they are meant to
be in that world. There is no insulation, no cushioning
from the harsh realities of life. The hope of heaven is
for real – but it does not shield us from the pain of this
present life. The suffering, crucifixion and resurrection

of Jesus Christ map out the shape of the true Christian
life. The only road that leads to hope passes through
suffering and death. From the perspective of the Road,
other routes may seem easier and more attractive – but
from the Balcony, they are seen to be dead ends.

To become a real Christian may also involve enter-
ing into suffering on account of faith itself. 'Christ
suffered for you, leaving you an example, that you
should follow in his steps' (1 Peter 2:21). It is to
take up a cross and follow Christ. Suffering is part
of the lot of the believer. 'Rejoice that you participate in the sufferings of Christ, so that you may be
overjoyed when his glory is revealed' (1 Peter 4:13).

So does this mean that Christians should seek out
suffering, so that they can be more like Christ? No.
Suffering comes our way in God's own good time, if it
comes at all. The time and place of suffering are best
left to the wisdom of God. What matters is how we view
that suffering, and how we are prepared to use it.

Some, like Job's misguided comforters, will always
insist that suffering is a mark of divine disfavour
or punishment. But responsible Christian theology
knows otherwise. From the Road, suffering looks like
unequivocally bad news. It seems to show that we
are cut off from the presence of God. But from the
Balcony, things look different. Suffering is seen as a
potential mark of God's favour and presence, as he
allows us the privilege in sharing in the suffering
of his own Son. Suffering is the same experience,
whether viewed from the Balcony or the Road – but it
is seen in a very different light, and with equally
different results. Those on the Road need the perspective of the Balconeers if they are, in the first place, to
cope with suffering and, in the second, to learn from
it.

Suffering does not mean that we are far from God; it
can mean that we are being drawn closer to him, and

are being allowed to go through an experience which can break down the remaining barriers between ourselves and him. It was through the bitter experience of a 'thorn in his flesh' that Paul learned that most important of all spiritual lessons – that the grace of God was sufficient for him, and that the power of God is made perfect in human weakness (2 Corinthians 12:7–10). As Martin Luther emphasised many times, suffering is a tool by which God can strip away our veneer of self-satisfaction and self-delusion, and help us to face up to our weakness and his strength.

But if the gospel means only suffering, in what sense is it good news? The Christian answer to this question is powerful, and needs to be heard carefully. Through faith, we are caught up in the life of Christ. We become united with Christ, and share in all that he is and achieves. A number of images are used within the Christian tradition to bring out the full richness of this theme: for example, Paul's use of the legal image of adoption.

This image is used by Paul to express the relation between believers and Jesus Christ (Romans 8:15; 8:23; 9:4; Galatians 4:5; Ephesians 1:5). Under Roman law, a father could adopt people from outside his natural family, and give them a legal status of adoption, thus placing them within the family. Although a distinction would still be possible between the natural and adopted children, they had the same legal status. In the eyes of the law, they were all members of the same family, irrrespective of their origins.

Paul deploys this image partly to indicate that, through faith, believers come to have the same status as Jesus, without implying that they possess the same divine nature as Jesus. Faith brings about a change in our status before God, incorporating us within the family of God, despite the fact that we do not share the same divine origins as Christ.

But he also makes use of the idea in another manner.
To be an adopted child is to share the same inheritance
rights as the natural children. As believers, we thus
inherit from God our Father, in much the same way
as Christ does. We are heirs of God, and co-heirs with
Christ. And what does this mean? <u>It means that we
can, in due course, expect to inherit everything that
Christ received as an inheritance from God.</u> And what
did Christ receive? According to Paul, in the first place
suffering, and in the second, glory. No suffering, no
glory. Through faith, we come to share in this pattern of
divine inheritance, mapped out for us by Christ: suffering, followed by glory (Romans 8:17; 1 Peter 3:12–14).

A second image is that of marriage, hinted at by
Paul, and, as we shall see, developed in the writings
of such thinkers as Martin Luther and John Calvin.
Faith is like a marriage bond. It unites two people
in a real and personal union. To be a Christian is
to be in Christ – that is, to be united through faith
to the risen Christ. And in marriage, a man and a
woman come together in a union which involves the
mutual sharing of goods. What belongs to the groom
is shared with the bride, just as what belongs to the
bride is shared with the groom.

To think of faith as a marriage between the believer and Christ thus emphasises the real and personal nature of the union between them. Faith is not
knowing about Christ; it is knowing Christ, and being
known by him. Faith is not about theories or ideas.
It is about personal relationships that transform us.
And it is about a real sharing between the believer
and Christ. But it is an unequal sharing. We give
Christ our sins and mortality. He bestows upon us
his righteousness and grace – and his earthly suffering
and heavenly glorification. These become ours through
faith. Every now and then, our pain may be transfigured by glimpses of his glory.

Suffering is part of a greater whole. It is the link between our present state of lowliness, and our future state of glory. Theology allows us to see suffering as a window into the presence of God, in that we see through it and beyond it, and catch a glimpse of the glory and presence of God which lies through its gateway. It cannot be avoided – but it need not be feared.

The New Testament is shot through with the idea that to become a Christian is to enter the experience of the suffering people of God, who are able to witness to God through that suffering, and draw nearer to him as a result of it. Perhaps the most moving statement of this belief can be found in 1 Peter. Christians are those who have been called out of darkness into God's wonderful light (2:9). Yet the world resents their presence and their calling, and inflicts suffering upon them as a result. 'Dear friends, do not be surprised at the painful trial you are suffering, as though something strange were happening to you. But rejoice that you participate in the sufferings of Christ, so that you may be overjoyed when his glory is revealed' (4:12–13). Suffering is not a sign of being outside the family of God, but a distinguishing mark of membership.

So to be united to Christ is to share in his sufferings, and to hope to share in his risen glory. To *hope* to share? Yes. Faith is about being able to see beyond the present life to that which lies thereafter. Present suffering will give way to future glory, as surely as Good Friday gave way to Easter Day. To those outside the Christian faith, who refuse to believe in anything beyond the present order of things, suffering can only be seen as an end. It has no possibility of being transformed. But the Christian knows of the transfiguration of suffering through resurrection – and so lives in hope. We shall explore this theme in our final chapter.

14

THE HOPE OF GLORY

Suffering and death, like sin, are hateful to God. Jesus
wept as he stood before the tomb of Lazarus, the same
Jesus who is none other than Immanuel, God with us –
God incarnate. Think of it: God cries over the death of
one of his creatures, whom he loves. The tears of Christ
are a powerful reminder of the compassion of our God
as we, like Lazarus, suffer and die.

John paints the most tender picture of Jesus, deeply
affected by the grief of Mary and Martha. I have often
wondered how best to translate the Greek text of John
11:33. Jesus is deeply moved; he is greatly upset; he
is perhaps even angry. About what? About the pain of
the human situation, and the grief that it occasions.
Suffering, death and sin are all part and parcel of our
tragic fallen human situation. It is important to affirm
the Christian hope and faith that the way things are is
not the way things are meant to be – nor the way they
shall remain.

Some say that nothing could ever be adequate rec-
ompense for suffering in this world. But how do they
know? Have they spoken to anyone who has suffered
and subsequently been raised to glory? Have they been
through this experience themselves? One of the greatest tragedies of much writing about human suffering this century has been its crude use of rhetoric.
'Nothing can ever compensate for suffering!' rolls off
the tongue with the greatest of ease. It has a certain

oratorical force. It discourages argument. It suggests that what has been said represents the distillation of human wisdom on the subject, and is so evidently correct that it does not require justification. It implies that anyone who disagrees is a fool. But how do they know that nothing can compensate for suffering? Paul believed passionately that the sufferings of the present life would be outweighed by the glory that is to come (Romans 8:18). How do they know that he is wrong, and that they are right?

Have they tasted the glory of the life to come, so that they can make the comparison? Have they talked to others who have been through the bitter experience of suffering and death, and have been caught up in the risen and glorious life of Christ, and asked them how they now feel about their past suffering? No. Of course they haven't. The simple truth is that this confident assertion of the critics of Christianity is just so much whistling in the wind. Their comments are made from our side of the veil which separates history from eternity.

Now the situation would be rather different if we could listen to someone who suffers a humiliating and painful death, and then returns to us from the dead. He would speak with authority and insight on this matter. It is here that the resurrection of Christ becomes of central importance. God has indeed spoken on such matters. We can know something of what lies ahead. We can see suffering from the perspective of eternity.

At the time of Christ, people expected a general resurrection at the end of time. It would mark the end of history, and was to be accompanied by divine judgement and the self-revelation of God. The resurrection of Christ was totally unexpected. It didn't fit any of the expected patterns of the time. It was as if something that was meant to happen at the end of time had taken place right in the middle of human history.

The resurrection thus allows the suffering of Christ to be seen from the perspective of eternity. Suffering is not pointless, but leads to glory. Those who share in the sufferings of Christ may, through the resurrection of Christ, know what awaits them at the end of history. It is for this reason that Paul is able to declare with such confidence that 'our present sufferings are not worth comparing with the glory that will be revealed in us' (Romans 8:18). This is no groundless hope, no arbitrary aspiration. It is a hard-headed realism, grounded in the reality of the suffering and resurrection of Christ, and the knowledge that faith binds us to Christ, and guarantees that we shall share in his heritage.

The New Testament affirms that sufferings of this earth are for real. They are painful. God is deeply pained by our suffering, just as we are shocked, grieved and mystified by the suffering of our family and friends. But that is only half of the story. The other half must be told. It is natural that our attention should be fixed upon what we experience and feel here and now. But faith demands that we raise our sights, and look to what lies ahead. We may suffer as we journey – but where are we going? What lies ahead?

The word 'heaven' seems inadequate to describe the final goal of faith. Perhaps we should speak more expansively of the hope of eternal life, of the renewing of our frail and mortal bodies in the likeness of Christ's glorious resurrection body, and the ultimate prize of standing, redeemed, in the presence of God. But, however we choose to describe it, the promise and hope of our transformation and renewal, and of the glorious transfiguration of suffering, are an integral part of the Christian faith. This glorious thread is woven so deeply into the fabric of our faith that it cannot possibly be removed.

The language of 'prizes' and 'rewards' is helpful in many ways. It reminds us of the need to complete the race, in order that we may receive the athlete's crown (2 Timothy 4:7–8). It reminds us of the need for training and discipline in the Christian life, to build up the stamina we need in order to persevere.

But this way of thinking about the relation between suffering and heaven can also be misleading. It implies an accidental connection between suffering and heaven. It suggests that heaven is thrown in as some kind of consolation, in order to keep us going here below. In his acclaimed sermon 'The Weight of Glory', C S Lewis addresses this question as follows:

> There are different kinds of reward. There is the reward which has no natural connection with the things you do to earn it, and is quite foreign to the desires that ought to accompany those things. Money is not the natural reward of love; that is why we call a man mercenary if he marries a woman for the sake of her money. But marriage is the proper reward for a real lover, and he is not mercenary for desiring it . . . The proper rewards are not simply tacked on to the activities for which they are given, but are the activity itself in consummation.

The danger identified by Lewis is easily avoided if we pay more attention to the intimacy of the connection between suffering and glory.

When a seed is planted in the ground, it begins to grow, and will eventually bear fruit. Can we say that its bearing fruit is a reward for its growth? No. We would say that there is an organic and natural connection between one and the other. That is just the way things are. It is not a question of declaring, in some arbitrary way, that a seed which grows will be rewarded with fruit, or that the prize for growth is fruit. Rather, we view germination, growth and the bearing of fruit as

all part of the same overall process. They are all stages
in the natural cycle of growth and development.

And so with suffering and glorification. They are
part of, but represent different stages within, the same
process of growth in the Christian life. We are adopted
into the family of God, we suffer, and we are glorified (Romans 8:14–18). This is not an accidental relationship. They are all intimately connected within
the overall pattern of Christian growth and progress
towards the ultimate goal of the Christian life – being
finally united with God, and remaining with him for
evermore. Heaven is the consummation of a process, of
which suffering is a present part.

We are thus presented with a glorious vision of a new
realm of existence. It is a realm in which suffering has
been defeated. It is a realm pervaded by the refreshing
presence of God, from which the presence and power of
sin have finally been excluded. It lies ahead, and we
have yet to enter into it, even if we can catch a hint
of its fragrance and hear its music in the distance.
It is this hope which keeps us going in this life of
sadness, which ends in death.

But is it for real? Is this hope anything more than
wishful thinking, a spurious pipedream, a pitiful hope
on the part of human beings who long for a better
world than that which they now know and inhabit?
We are all familiar with the tedious taunt of believing in 'pie in the sky when you die'. The implication
would seem to be that Christians are so deluded and
unrealistic about life that they need such fictional mor-
sels to keep them going, where others can cope with the
grim realities of life unaided.

But this evades the question. Is it true? If it is true,
Christians can hardly be criticised for believing in it.
If it is true, to ignore it is to run away from reality.
Either it is true, or it is not. So which is it? Let us
be absolutely clear on this. If the Christian hope of

heaven is an illusion, based upon lies, then it must be abandoned as misleading and deceitful. But if it is true, it must be embraced and allowed to transfigure our entire understanding of the place of suffering in life.

I believe it is for real, and that it is impossible for a Christian to discuss suffering without reference to it. Through the grace of God, suffering gives way to glory, as a woman's pain in childbirth gives way to the joy of new birth. And the Christian hope of heaven is deeply embedded within the gospel. It is not some add-on feature, some optional extra which got tacked on to the gospel at a later stage, which can be discarded at will. As I stressed earlier, it is part of an overall pattern of growth and development, comparable to the germination of a seed, leading to the growth and final coming to fruit of the resulting plant. It is an integral part of the gospel package, being totally consistent with the overall thrust of the proclamation of redemption in Christ.

The most helpful analogy for understanding this vital point is that of a human marriage, with faith being seen as analogous to the marriage bond uniting husband and wife. The German writer Martin Luther states this principle in his 1520 writing, *The Liberty of a Christian*:

Faith unites the soul with Christ as a bride is united with her bridegroom. As Paul teaches us, Christ and the soul become one flesh by this mystery (Ephesians 5:31–2). And if they are one flesh, and if the marriage is for real . . . then it follows that everything that they have is held in common, whether good or evil. So the believer can boast of and glory in whatever Christ possesses, as though it were his or her own. And whatever the believer has, Christ claims as his own. Let us see how this works out, and see how it benefits us. Christ is full of grace, life and salvation. The

> human soul is full of sin, death and damnation.
> Now let faith come between them. Sin, death and
> damnation will be Christ's. And grace, life and
> salvation will be the believer's.

A human marriage is no legal fiction. It is a real
and vital relationship between two persons, involving
personal union, mutual commitment, a common life
and a sharing of goods. Precisely this relationship is
established between the believer and the risen Christ
through faith.

The believer thus comes to be in Christ. He or she
is a new creation. A dynamic bond is forged between
the believing human being and the redeeming Christ,
bringing in its wake a partaking of all that he won
for us by his obedience. But whereas death eventually
parts a human couple, nothing – not even death itself –
can destroy the union between Christ and the believer.
It is for real, and it is for ever. Indeed, death merely
snaps the final surly bonds which link us with the un-
redeemed world of sin, enabling us to commit ourselves
totally and unreservedly to Christ.

The believer thus shares in Christ's victory over
death, his breaking free from the bonds of suffering
and pain, and his risen life. Christians are assured
that they will share in this resurrection, and will share
the life of the risen, ascended and glorified Christ.
The victory over sin is only complete when we are
saved, not merely from its penalty and power, but also
from its presence. Here the great promises of the Old
Testament find their final fulfilment. We are brought
into the presence of God, rejoicing.

This, then, is the hope of faith. Hope! How much
spiritual excitement and depth is compressed into that
single word. This is no shallow optimism, no vague
and uniformed wish that all might turn out well, when
everything indicates it will not. 'I hope that George

won't make a fool of himself again tonight.' 'I hope it will stop raining soon.' No. <u>Here is a sure and confident expectation, born of the trustworthiness of God, nourished by his promises and sustained by the gracious working of the Holy Spirit.</u>

This sure anticipation of our future union with God allows us to yearn passionately to be with God, to crave for his closer presence, and to view this life in the light of this final goal. Just as a soldier fights on towards the end of a long war, sustained by the knowledge that peace will one day come, and he will be reunited with his family and friends, so the Christian continues his pilgrimage, sustained by the knowledge of the joys that await him.

Karl Marx regarded this outlook on life as little more than nauseating sentimentality. By offering us hope for the future, it distracted us from changing the world for the better. The promise of the final removal of suffering and pain in the kingdom of God distracted us from working for their elimination here and now. To use Marx's famous phrase, Christianity is 'an opiate for the masses', a kind of anaesthetic or narcotic which dulls our senses, and prevents us from doing something about the shameful situation of our world.

Now Marx has a fair point. So great is the attractiveness of the Christian hope that it is natural to become fascinated by it, and to want to focus our thoughts upon it. It is all too easy to become so heavenly minded as to be of no earthly use. <u>If Marx's criticism serves any useful purpose, it is to remind us that we have a Christian duty to work for the transformation of the world as we know it, removing the causes of unnecessary suffering.</u> The Christian hope ought to be a stimulus, rather than a sedative. It should spur us to action within the world, rather than encourage us to neglect it. By working to lessen the suffering of God's world and his people, we are easing his heartache over their pain.

But when all is said and done, Marx's comment merely reinforces the power and importance of the Christian hope. It *does* enable us to cope with suffering in the present life. That is at one and the same time both its danger and its attractiveness. Precisely because it so successfully enables us to cope with the turmoil and sorrow of the world, it could tempt us to leave them unaltered. Marx is thus a reluctant, yet eloquent, witness to the power of the Christian hope to enable us to cope with the dark side of life.

So how does this hope console us? By setting our present situation in its full context. By allowing eternity to break in to time and illuminate it. By reminding and reassuring us that 'our present sufferings are not worth comparing with the glory that will be revealed in us.' (Romans 8:18). By calling to our memory those great figures of the past who, by faith, reached out to receive the same hope, without the benefit of the firm assurances given to us through Christ that these promises would find their fulfilment (Hebrews 11:1–40).

Are we frightened by death? Faith assures us that to die is to gain, and to be with the Christ we long to know fully. Are we troubled by sorrow? Faith tells us of another country – which is to be *our* country – where sorrow is no more, and where all tears have been wiped away. Do we suffer? Faith tells us of a time when death shall be swallowed up in victory, and the sufferings of the present day will seem insignificant in comparison with the joy that awaits us. And how great those sufferings are for so many. Is it not consoling to trust that the bliss of heaven will exceed them, both in intensity and duration?

Just as suffering is real, so are the promises of God and the hope of eternal life. The death and resurrection of Christ, linked with the giving of the Holy Spirit, are pledges, sureties and guarantees that what has been promised will one day be brought to glorious realisation. For the moment we struggle and suffer in sadness mingled with bewilderment. But one day, all that will be changed for the people of God:

> God himself will be with them and be their God. He will wipe every tear from their eyes. There will be no more death or mourning or crying or pain, for the old order of things has passed away' (Revelation 21:3–4).

In that hope, we go forward into life in faith. We may not know exactly where that faith will lead us. But we do know that, wherever we go, the God of all compassion goes ahead of us and journeys with us, consoling and reassuring us, until that day when we shall see him face to face, and know him as he knows us.

BIBLE PASSAGES
TO STUDY

It is enormously helpful to reflect on some key biblical passages about suffering. What follows are some of the most important, along with brief introductions which may be of use to you as you study them.

Romans 8:16–18. Paul declares that Christians share in all the privileges of being children of God. Just as Christ suffered before being raised to glory, so believers must expect to do the same. Note how Paul argues that such sufferings will be seen in their true light once we have been raised to glory, and can look back on them from this perspective.

Romans 8:28. Here Paul affirms that God is working out his good purposes in all that we experience, even if we cannot fully understand what is happening.

Romans 8:35–9. In this powerful passage Paul declares that nothing in all of creation can separate believers from the love of God in Christ. We may not be able to understand the place that suffering, pain or hardship may play within the overall purposes of God, but we can be sure that the love of God for us will remain and will finally triumph.

2 Corinthians 1:3–7. Paul stresses the wonderful compassion of God for believers, reassuring his readers that suffering is an integral part of the Christian life. Note how the sufferings of Christ on the cross are given pride of place.

Hebrews 12:7–8. This passage emphasises that the discipline of suffering is to be seen as a privilege of being the children of God. What may seem incomprehensible to us may be the way in which God is guiding and building us up.

1 Peter 1:6–7. Peter here notes how suffering is a way in which God refines our faith, removing its impurities. Notice how Peter declares that the faith of believers is worth more than gold.

1 Peter 2:19–23. Here Peter points out that being a Christian involves going through the same sufferings as Christ.

Revelations 21:1–5. This great passage offers us a vision of the New Jerusalem, from which all pain and suffering have been banished. This passage has been of enormous value to Christians thinking about the pain of suffering, looking ahead with hope to its final removal in the life to come.